How To Make
Big Money in
Multi-Level Marketing

How To Make Big Money in Multi-Level Marketing

Dave Roller

PRENTICE HALL
Englewood Cliffs, New Jersey 07632

Prentice-Hall International (UK) Limited, *London*
Prentice-Hall of Australia, Pty. Limited, *Sydney*
Prentice-Hall Canada, Inc., *Toronto*
Prentice-Hall Hispanoamericana, S.A., *Mexico*
Prentice-Hall of India Private Limited, *New Delhi*
Prentice-Hall of Japan, Inc., *Tokyo*
Simon & Schuster Asia Pte Ltd., *Singapore*
Editora Prentice-Hall do Brasil, Ltda., *Rio de Janeiro*

© 1989 *by*
Prentice-Hall, Inc.
Englewood Cliffs, New Jersey 07632

Printed in the United States of America

10   9   8   7   6   5   4   3   2   1

Library of Congress Cataloging-in-Publication Data

Roller, Dave,
    How to make big money in multi-level marketing / Dave Roller.
      p.   cm.
    Includes index.
    ISBN 0-13-417858-0.—ISBN 0-13-417866-1 (pbk)
    1. Multilevel marketing. I. Title.
    HF5415.126.R64   1989
  658.8′4—dc19   88-37639
                                              CIP

ISBN 0-13-417858-0

ISBN 0-13-417866-1 (PBK)

PRENTICE HALL
BUSINESS & PROFESSIONAL DIVISION
A division of Simon & Schuster
Englewood Cliffs, New Jersey 07632

This book is dedicated to
my wife
Billie
for the Love, Joy, and Support
she brings into my life
and to our children
Amanda
Jennifer
David, Jr. (D.J.)
Linda
Scott
Steve

Contents

This Book Will:

1. Help you to see how MLM can create a dynamic income for you.
2. Show you how MLM can be used for fund raising.
3. Give you a formula for a fast start.
4. Teach you conference call recruiting.
5. Provide you a word-for-word script on how to respond when prospects answer your ad.
6. Give you a script on how to set appointments.
7. Teach you the Spare Tire principle, the Ten Balloon principle, the 3–30–300 principle, and 16 other principles that will work for you.
8. Instruct you on how to duplicate yourself by delegating.
9. Give you proven ideas for better communication.
10. Provide you with special tips to hold successful opportunity meetings.
11. Give you rules to follow for better recruiting.
12. Teach you the "farm system" of prospecting for new customers.
13. Teach you a simple and effective approach for asking for referrals.
14. Give you word pictures that move others to action.
15. Instruct you on how to deal with excuses.
16. Show you how to revive a "dead" organization.
17. Teach you how to keep yourself from burning out.

18. Prove to you that you *do* have a choice.

19. Help you to overcome discouragement.

People who want to earn more money often make a common mistake. They assume they must do something difficult, disagreeable, or expensive, like earn still another college degree, sell their soul to the company they work for, or invest tens of thousands of dollars to buy a franchise.

There are many people today who are selling themselves short by continually accepting assignments they don't like, moving when and where the company says (never mind that your spouse and children don't want to move any more than you do), learning to play petty company politics, or mortgaging the security of their homes for some high-risk investment or franchise opportunity.

All this to (a) hopefully earn a "big" income someday and (b) to retire on a "big" pension when you reach your sixties.

But there is another way that is simple, can be a lot of fun, and makes it possible for you to earn an extremely high income through the free enterprise system. It's called "multi-level marketing" or "network marketing."

How to Make Big Money in Multi-Level Marketing provides the ideas and inspiration to assist you to develop financial freedom in your life.

As Percy Whiting, an assistant to Dale Carnegie once wrote, "Any fool can learn from experience. It takes a smart salesman to learn from a book . . . and it pays."

Introduction

One of the most misunderstood concepts in America today is multi-level marketing, sometimes called "network marketing."

Multi-level marketing (MLM) is a multibillion dollar industry that is growing larger every day. Literally thousands of people are developing financial freedom *now* in multi-level marketing, with incomes of $25,000 to $50,000 and more per year. Many incomes exceed $100,000 per year, and some earn over $1 million per year in MLM.

This is not a rah-rah, you-can-do-it-too type of book. This book contains no-nonsense, practical suggestions from a highly successful MLM expert, Dave Roller. He will share with you techniques that have proven successful. These techniques have worked well for him and many others, and they can work well for you, too, as you learn and apply them in your business.

Because the ideas are simple, down-to-earth, and workable, you will find this book highly motivational. If you don't already understand the dynamics of multi-level marketing, don't worry, because you will as you read this book. *How to Make Big Money in Multi-Level Marketing* will help you to appreciate what a good MLM opportunity can do for you!

How To Make
Big Money in
Multi-Level Marketing

Chapter
1

HOW TO PROSPER AND ENJOY THE GOOD LIFE THROUGH MULTI-LEVEL MARKETING

Here is an amazing fact: in the United States, one household in 100 has a net worth of $1 million or more. Today there are almost a million millionaires!

Meanwhile, countless people in less-than-wealthy circumstances ask, "What must I do to acquire more money and enjoy the life style that comes with it? How can I achieve greater happiness, prosperity, and satisfaction in my life?"

This book will help you, regardless of your age, sex, education, family, background, health, or occupation, make the transition from where you *are* to where you *want* to be.

According to many marketing experts, 80 percent of today's millionaires "made it" in the last 20 years. And they are wealthy in nonmonetary ways, too. Most of today's financially successful people enjoy hard work, place top emphasis on their families, and are well respected.

Consider these examples of ordinary folks who are enjoying extraordinary, even awesome, rewards through networking.

A Kansas couple discovered an MLM opportunity and within three years were earning over $80,000 per year.

A Florida multimillionaire bought a service sold by a networking friend. Another business friend of hers from another state was in a career change, and she mentioned the MLM opportunity to him. He became interested, and within just two years his MLM organization had grown so successful that his friend in Florida now receives more than $70,000 per year income from the venture. She says this was the best $100 business investment she ever made!

A railroad conductor living in a small home in Georgia saw a chance for freedom in his life through multi-level marketing. Within eight years his income grew from $18,000 to over $1 million per year.

A policeman from upstate New York discovered networking in his living room. Ten years later, he and his wife enjoy two homes on the ocean and the financial freedom to travel and vacation whenever and wherever they please.

A Filipino couple immigrated to Arizona. They opened their own business, but financial difficulties forced them to discontinue it. One day they answered an ad for an MLM opportunity. They now earn over $10,000 per month, enabling them to spend more time with their children, and this was accomplished in just a few short years.

There's a famous former New York Yankee who doesn't miss the high income of a major league baseball player who pitched in the World Series because his networking income is well over half a million dollars per year.

There are literally thousands of people discovering a good life of prosperity through MLM throughout the United States, England, Canada, Australia, Japan, Germany, France, and many more countries today.

This book examines a new, exciting, and growing business system. Its purpose is not to sell you a specific company. Rather, *How to Make Big Money in Multi-Level Marketing* explains how MLM works, answers your questions, outlines the future of the industry, and helps you decide whether the concept holds promise for you.

What Is Multi-Level Marketing?

Multi-level or network marketing is a system by which a parent company distributes its services or products through a network of independent business people, not only in the United States but throughout the free world. These independent business people or entrepreneurs then sponsor other people to help them distribute the product or service. This people-helping-people process may be continued through one or more levels of earnings.

As a networker you can earn money in two ways:

1. You distribute the service or product you are handling to your friends and to clients who are referred to you.

2. You invite friends and others you meet to explore an opportunity to also distribute your product or service.

The extent to which you involve yourself with either or both of these two activities depends strictly upon your personal preferences. Some people concentrate on distributing the services and products. These people, then, are limited to their personal efforts. There are others who not only market an MLM product, but also learn how to sponsor and build up a large organization. Those who persist in sponsoring can greatly "multiply" themselves by helping others to grow.

This multiplication effect is the magic of multi-level marketing. There are only 24 hours in a day, but by learning how to sponsor others, you can duplicate your efforts as you add to your income, yet have nobody on your payroll. You can actually earn money while you sleep.

Multi-level marketing has been around since the early 1950s, but is still considered to be in its infancy. As more people understand its mechanics, however, MLM will become an increasingly popular method of distribution.

For example, one innovative networking company proved that a largely part-time sales organization built through multi-level marketing could become the world's leading life insurance company within just ten years.

A Michigan-based corporation started in 1959 was doing over $1 billion per year in sales through its MLM organization just 15 years later. This same company now approaches $2 billion per year in sales worldwide.

A California family decided to market its nutritional program of vitamins and minerals through multi-level marketing. What a success story this corporation has become! It is now listed on the New York Stock Exchange, and its products are marketed worldwide.

There are a number of successful MLM companies, but it is not always best to be swayed into a new idea touted as a ground-floor opportunity. It is sometimes more sensible to build with a solid, proven opportunity where you have support.

When considering an MLM company, it is important to realize that, as in any industry, there are companies that begin and fail soon after.

If you are considering a newer, unproved company, ask to see audited financial records as you would with any other business opportunity.

Why I Joined MLM
Dick and JoAnn Campbell, Michigan

My first reaction to multi-level marketing was that it was a pyramid scheme. The only reason I went to a meeting was to protect a friend of mine from being taken in.

The opposite happened, and I became impressed with what I saw. I discovered that multi-level marketing was not only a legitimate way to earn money, but possibly the best way for many people to make a living.

As a college professor, I was committed to helping others obtain their college degrees to get ahead in life. With MLM, I'm still a teacher. The main difference is that people do not need to pay tuition and go to college for four years. They can master it on a part-time basis and make more income part time than most college graduates who work a full-time job.

MLM is the great equalizer—anyone can succeed. It doesn't matter how old you are, what your race or sex is, or whether you're rich or poor. And it doesn't matter what you've done before. The only concern is where you want to go from here and whether or not you are willing to make the effort to achieve.

What's the Future for Networking?

There are only a few giant MLM organizations today. Multi-level marketing will become a major trend in marketing during the next decade. The networking system of distribution will be applied to an ever-increasing variety of products and services.

In recent years MLM companies have become leaders in household products, synthetic motor oils, personal care products, and some forms of insurance, along with a variety of other products and services. In the future we will see MLM emerge as a leading system in marketing investment, securities, real estate, travel, and perhaps even medical services. As more people gain experience in networking, they will discover how to apply it to more products and services.

The friends-doing-business-with-friends method of distribution is limited only by people's imaginations and initiative. It is fascinating that, for an investment of normally less than $100, you can join a solid MLM company and possibly end up with a worldwide marketing organization.

Which Is Better, Franchising or Multi-Level Marketing?

Franchising is sometimes compared with multi-level marketing, but the two systems are quite different. Both are relatively new distribution methods, both capitalize on the talents and energies of entrepreneurs, and both have created many millionaires.

Franchising is a system whereby someone develops a product or service and then licenses or franchises it to franchisees for a price plus a percentage of all the revenues the franchisee takes in. Henry Ford was one of the first major franchisers, using the method to build a dealer network shortly after the turn of the century. In more recent times, franchising has been the secret to the fantastic success of McDonald's, Kentucky Fried Chicken, Holiday Inn, and hundreds of other internationally known distributors of products and services.

But franchising, great as it is as a way to make money for both the franchiser and franchisee, has drawbacks, particularly for a fledgling entrepreneur. The first is cost. Successful franchises are expensive. Unless you can put your hands on $50,000 or more, forget about buying a fast-food franchise. And unless you can come up with at least a million, forget about buying a motel franchise.

A second drawback to franchising is that not everyone qualifies. Even if money is no problem, unless you can meet certain standards (credit history, business experience, etc.) the best-known franchisers will not sell you the right to do business under their name.

Finally, some entrepreneurs do not like the nearly absolute conformity to standardized operating procedures franchisers typically impose.

On the other hand, multi-level marketing lets an entrepreneur get started with very little capital, usually under $100, and the network marketer, unlike the franchisee, has no expensive buildings to pay for, requires no staff, and is allowed maximum freedom in deciding how to manage his or her business.

What Must I Invest to Succeed Big?

The axiom "Nothing ventured, nothing gained" is true in multi-level marketing just as it is in all facets of business and nonbusiness life.

If you invest or plant nothing, you gain or harvest nothing. If you don't plant money in a savings account, you won't harvest interest. And if you don't invest in a stock, you cannot harvest a dividend. Granted, some people *think* they can amass a fortune without planting the seeds that grow a fortune, but the truth is they cannot. If nothing is ventured, nothing is gained. And if someone promises you riches without investing what it takes to produce riches, they are simply trying to deceive you.

Why I Joined MLM
Doug Vandiford, Georgia

I first saw multi-level marketing when I was graduating from college with a degree in computer programming. I was excited about the opportunity to sponsor others and the opportunity to earn money. MLM later gave me the financial springboard to go into real estate ventures and to serve in politics for two terms in the Georgia House of Representatives.

Many people are looking for a quick and easy way to make money in life, and there just isn't such a way. It takes a while to build a solid business. But, by sticking to the basics, it can be done. Because of the continuing income with MLM, you can have security and peace of mind in your life.

> Anyone can do this business if they will only do the following three things:
> 1. Work seriously at the business
> 2. Find a quality product that performs a quality service
> 3. Find a company with a well-balanced marketing plan geared toward longevity

Success in MLM requires you to make a six-part investment:

1. *A token amount of money, usually less than $100.* MLM is the least capital-intensive business you can get into. This is good news for entrepreneurs, because hundreds of university and government studies show that lack of capital is, by far, the number-one reason why businesses fail.

Look at what you *don't need* to get into MLM:

a. You don't need to purchase a big inventory, tools, or equipment.

b. You don't need to rent, buy, or lease a building.

c. You don't need to hire employees.

d. You don't need to pay a big franchise fee for the right to do business. (Most such fees range from $10,000 to $250,000.)

e. You don't need to purchase good will.

There is another big cost advantage. Most MLM people keep their regular jobs and operate their business part-time. Money you earn from your networking business is pure profit. In most other entrepreneurial businesses, you must give up the job you originally had. In networking you come close to having your cake and eating it too.

2. *Eagerness to learn the business.* While all MLM plans are similar, each has its unique features. A willingness to learn what specific tactics work best shortens the time required to earn substantial money. The point here is to seek out successful associates in your MLM business and *ask questions.*

Multi-level marketing is structured such that you are a learner and a teacher at the same time. Your sponsor and/or upline will teach you the business and help you deal with problems successfully. Most networking organizations hold training seminars and motivational rallies, supply you with idea literature and encouragement, and provide any other as-sistance you need to succeed.

3. *Creative enthusiasm* is the third investment you must make for big success in networking.

Many businesses (such as franchises, automobile sales, retail sales, and chemical production) are *capital intensive,* meaning enormous money is required for success. Other busi-nesses are *labor intensive,* meaning the major investment re-quired is money to hire labor, as in restaurants, medical care facilities, and auto repair shops.

Multi-level marketing, on the other hand, is *enthusiasm intensive,* meaning that your desire to succeed, backed by your commitment, is critically important.

Your sponsor or mentor will give you the assistance you need to master the fundamentals, if you ask for his or her help. You will normally find the encouragement to use your creative talent to build your business.

Franchise systems require the franchisee to follow an ex-actly prescribed marketing plan. In multi-level marketing, your sponsor will suggest how you can build your business, but you will have more personal freedom to service customers and op-erate your business.

Being creative in multi-level marketing will help you to find new, better, easier, and simpler ways to achieve your goal of success. Early on you learn there is no one best way to do any task—there are as many "best ways" as there are good people. What is important is that you find a way that works best for you.

Multi-level marketing gives you a chance to try *your* ideas for making money, *your* techniques for leading and managing people, and *your* approach to problem solving. You can count on other people for advice, assistance, and help, but ultimately *you* make most of the decisions that relate to your business—how to sell, recruit, and motivate people, where to operate (some networkers operate their businesses on every conti-nent), and how much time you want to invest.

4. *A strong desire to help others succeed* is the fourth part of your investment in networking success. Wanting to show others how they can earn more money is important because

you succeed in direct proportion to your ability to help other
people succeed. Your ability to help other people succeed will
be in proportion to your commitment to building your business. Multi-level marketing is a business opportunity. The saying "Anything worth having is worth working for" aptly applies to the MLM industry.

Your downline organization will need you for guidance,
development, and know-how. You need them for their sales
production and to help make your network family grow. As is
explained later, the larger your family of associates grows, the
larger your income will be.

The essence of networking is people helping people. Successful networkers *want* to show others how to get started in
the business, achieve financial success, and make dreams come
true. Sure, the financial rewards for you can be excellent, but
you will also enjoy showing other people how they can earn
money to pay for their child's braces or pay off their debts or
buy a bigger home. Successful networkers take joy in helping
others make money to invest, develop a second income, and
enjoy their free time.

5. *The expenditure of some of your free time* is the fifth
part of your investment. The only asset everyone has in equal
amounts is time. Each of us—successes and failures, rich or
poor, young or old, employed and unemployed—has exactly
24 hours a day, 168 hours a week.

How large a time investment you make in your networking business is up to you. Many MLM newcomers begin with
only ten to 15 hours per week. Others find that by giving up
some TV time they can easily invest 20 to 25 hours a week.

In multi-level marketing you duplicate your efforts by
bringing others into the business. This means that your weekly
personal time investment of 15 hours could multiply into 100 or
even 1,000 hours per week in production. The activity created
by your downline organization duplicates over and over again
the time that you invested. And this duplication results in multiplying your income.

Successful people know that each of us can find time for
what we really want to do. And, since most of us really want to
make more money, making the time investment is no problem.

6. *Handling problems.* Along the way in your MLM career you will encounter some problems. This is not a negative statement, but simply a fact of life. How you approach and handle these challenges will determine how large your business will ultimately grow.

Even though you are technically an independent contractor, you do have a relationship with certain other leaders (normally in your upline) for support and assistance. It is important that you use good judgment and common sense when choosing a mentor with whom to align you and your organization.

Why? You may, for example, be encouraged to purchase a large product inventory that is not yet necessary. This is an expensive investment that you may never see a return on. Reputable MLM companies work to the best of their abilities to police those few who create these types of problems, but it is important to exercise common sense in controlling your business investment and expenses.

Why I Joined MLM
Nancy Brown, New Hampshire

I went from failing my real-estate exam three times before finally passing it to selling $23 million worth of real estate in four and a half years!

When I first discovered multi-level marketing, I was already successful, but I saw that it offered me flexibility and freedom. I like to *go* and to *do*, and I enjoy working with people from all walks of life.

Many times when you build others up in the conventional business world, they end up with your job! In multi-level marketing, when you build others up, *they* can achieve the same level of incentive that *you* do—but *you* always continue to benefit!

As a career, multi-level marketing has far fewer problems than franchising and other business opportunities simply because of the fact that you do not need employees. In MLM, good assistance is there—if you seek it out.

There are no promotions based on how well a boss likes you. Networking is structured to reward one's own initiative and the ambition to succeed. Relatives of the boss have no advantages. And no one gets more because of seniority.

In networking you'll meet people from every conceivable background—school teachers, professional athletes, engineers, factory workers, administrators, mechanics, dentists, judges, clerks, professors, secretaries, students, executives, military officers, physicians, homemakers, ministers, and airline pilots.

A cardinal premise of networking is that everyone starts equal. You can't buy your way to a higher level. Your performance and *only* your performance determines how well you are rewarded. Remember, in network marketing, every advancement you make, every check you receive, every reward you get, every time you are singled out for recognition, is squarely for what you have developed through personal and downline efforts.

Make no mistake, the business environment has changed. Today, experts in conventional businesses design compensation plans to severely restrict the number of persons who can make $100,000 or more. In 1986, less than 1 percent of corporate employees earned six figures. And all too frequently the company that looks as if it will prosper doesn't, and its pension plan goes bottom up too. Guarantees are gone. Corporate life expectancy is shortened. Consumer wants are more fickle. The only certainty is uncertainty—unless you control your economic future.

If you are to enjoy a large income, financial security, and the "good life," you can do it in your own business *now* more than at any other time in history.

Multi-level marketing, which is free enterprise in its purest form, carries no guarantees of big income and rapid wealth accumulation. But it does have an amazing record of helping ordinary folks earn substantial incomes. Clearly, American business has entered a new era. Networking is the closest we have come to what the nation's founders had in mind—that people who work hard, exercise personal leadership, serve others exceptionally well, and accept responsibility *should be handsomely rewarded*. But those who do no more than is required, worship the clock, avoid initiative, and expect Uncle

Sam, the union, Santa Claus, or a state lottery to provide them with a first-class standard of living are in for a shock.

Jobs have changed a great deal in the past 20 years, but most of them still have one characteristic they had in 1960, 1920, or 1850: most of them are still dead-end. Of the thousands of people who go to work every day for big corporations, only a small percentage can expect to be president of the company someday. In multi-level marketing you can become the president of your own marketing organization today!

Millions of people go through life never discovering what they can do, how much they can earn, how good they really are. Networking gives a person the opportunity to use his or her abilities, talent, energy, and personality in an economic experiment that will in time tell you what stuff you're made of.

In the chapters that follow, I explain the essentials you need to be successful in multi-level marketing. Keep in mind that we are discussing networking as a system and only, incidentally, specific multi-level programs. Remember, knowledge is *not* power, power is knowledge put to use.

> *Whoever acquires knowledge but does not practice it, is as one*
> *who ploughs but does not sow.*
>
> *Saadi*

There is plenty of advice available on how to invest your money. The problem most people face is, Where do I get the money to invest? This book is about how to make money, not how to invest or spend it.

I will show you how to build an MLM business from scratch, step by step. Specifically, I explain:

1. How to start your own MLM marketing organization
2. How money is made in networking
3. The basics of making big money in MLM
4. How to bring together people to help you build your business
5. How to help your people succeed (remember, in MLM you succeed in proportion to how well your people succeed)
6. How to overcome the excuses people may give you for not joining your enterprise

7. Tax and other special advantages of networking
8. Methods for building your business nationally—even worldwide

MLM Success Profile:
The George and DeDe Shaw Story

George Shaw's father, the late Art Shaw, was one of the nation's leading harness drivers, so it was natural for George, a Bradley University graduate, to become interested in the business of harness racing. George and his wife, DeDe, developed more than 150 limited partners in their harness business and became the largest single importer of New Zealand horses in the United States.

One day George and DeDe began looking ahead and realized that, in the harness business, the only ones who were going to retire one day were the horses!

They began searching for a different opportunity. They considered a large investment in a pizza franchise that included the marketing rights for the state of New Jersey. During this time, they were using the Shaklee food supplements. When they saw the MLM opportunity that Shaklee offered, they saw that they could develop income not only in New Jersey, but throughout the United States, and other countries as well. The Shaws saw the potential of a large income, retirement, bonus cars, travel, and financial freedom, *without* the large financial investment required in franchising.

The Shaws' income grew from $484,424 their fifth year in business to $567,446 the sixth year and again increased to $744,645 their seventh year in multi-level marketing—more income and more freedom than most franchise owners ever hope to attain!

George and DeDe say, "We have friends all over the United States, and we can control how many days a week we work. If we please, we only work four days a week, and we take three off with our son A.G.

"We have enjoyed fabulous trips to San Francisco, The Bahamas, Aruba, Hawaii, Paris, Monte Carlo, Germany, Denmark, Australia, Montreal, Holland, and Switzerland, as well as a Caribbean cruise," continued the Shaws, "and all expenses were paid for the entire family by the company."

The Shaws presently drive two Cadillac bonus cars provided through their company's incentive plan.

George and DeDe enjoy the opportunity that multi-level marketing provides to work together as a husband–wife team. They say, "We have always kept our dreams high. You have to discipline yourself not to bring your dreams down to your income, but instead, to always reach higher."

George and DeDe's Keys to Success

Keep going no matter what happens, and help others with their needs. Don't worry about the people who say no. Concentrate on keeping your energy *focused on your goals*.

It is important to support each other as a husband–wife team. We find it important to set goals in life, but the goals have to be realistic. We learned from the harness-racing business to set a master goal, a major game plan. Then we set incremental goals that lead us step by step to our master goal.

The right attitude combined with the right thinking will lead you to success in your business. Keep updating your training. We find we cannot help people to be successful unless they want to help themselves. We ask new people to do the following:

1. Establish a commitment of time to their business.
2. Use and evaluate the products.
3. Form a game plan. This includes making a list of everyone they know, and then to come up with a top-ten hit list.
4. Attend weekly meetings.
5. Use audio and videotapes. We ask our people to follow a 6 × 6 plan, which is to give out one videotape per day for six weeks. We teach them to say, "This is my company's new videotape, and I would like you to see it and evaluate it. I will pick it up in 48 hours."
6. Graph a new associate's progress.
7. Run newspaper ads.

A big key to our success is to communicate with the people in our downline and help as many as possible to reach their goals. By helping other people to achieve what they want in life, ultimately, with the duplication of multi-level marketing, *our* goals are achieved.

You will have your ups and downs along with plateaus. You may also have doubts. But time and persistence are major keys to continual growth. The backbone of your MLM business is to talk to people every day. The cream always comes to the top, but you have to keep milking until it does.

We have found that joining a company that has credibility is important to your success in multi-level marketing. The Shaklees had been in business for more than 25 years when we joined them.

Our philosophy is "Do unto others as you would have them do unto you."

Chapter
2

HOW MULTI-LEVEL MARKETING WORKS

Maybe this chapter would be better titled "How Multi-Level Marketing Can Work for *You*." The concept of MLM or networking allows you to multiply your own efforts. It is a simple system whereby you can have hundreds or even thousands of others adding to your income, yet no one is on your payroll!

The concept of multi-level marketing is actually very simple. And for each of you who will learn the mechanics of multi-level marketing, you will discover that it can be a very effective and efficient marketing system.

Many people, though, do not or will not accept the opportunity as it is. This is probably because our human nature has been influenced by past experience to look at a product or service from a sales viewpoint. People instinctively want to know *who sells* the product and *how* the product is sold.

It is important to understand that you, when you were a student in school, were trained throughout your school years to "work a job." You are conditioned by the educational system to look for a career *as an employee*.

Most of us can only think in terms of earning money from our individual efforts. We don't normally envision ourselves leading others and earning a profit through *their* efforts as well—unless we are influenced outside the traditional educational system.

Napolean Hill states, "You become what you think you can become." Most of you have traditionally thought only about working for others. In many cases, multi-level marketing is the first time you have seen a way that you can multiply your own efforts.

Multi-level marketing allows you to duplicate yourself in others and end up multiplying your efforts. This is not much different from being the athletic director of a college sports program. As the athletic director you will recruit (sponsor) a head coach for various teams in your sports program. With your football team, for example, you will recruit and hire a head coach. To find your head coach, you will interview many different people before deciding on the one you want to work with in your football program, Right?

Well, it is similar in multi-level marketing. In MLM you will also interview and show them the opportunity you offer in order to find the few you are actually going to work with.

Once you have found your head football coach, he in turn, will recruit a head offensive coach and a head defensive coach. As the A.D., you most likely will be involved in assisting your head coach in finding and selecting his offensive and defensive coaches. You will most likely participate in some of these meetings, helping to build the dream of what your college sports program has to offer these coaches. You will help them to realize that the opportunity at your college is a good one for them. It is similar in multi-level marketing. You assist those you sponsor in recruiting their first-level associates. Your first-level associates in turn recruit associates for themselves. In multi-level marketing you benefit financially from not only these second-level associates, but also from third-level associates and sometimes beyond that.

As an upline sponsor, you participate in some of the meetings helping to share the dream of what your MLM company has to offer. Just like the A.D., you encourage the prospects to realize that the opportunity with your company is an excellent one for them. Furthermore, it is imperative that as an A.D. you support your head coach's efforts in recruiting good assistant coaches. The success of *his job* and *your job* depends on everyone's combined efforts in achieving the best results possible.

The A.D. and head football coach "profit" through the efforts of his assistant coaches—just as you and your first-level associates "profit" through the efforts of your downline MLM organization.

It's as one successful MLM person said, "An important key to multi-level marketing is to treat this business *as* a business. Pretend that your MLM business is an expensive franchise, treat it as such, and you will more likely be successful."

> ### Why I Joined MLM
> #### Ron Krueger, Wisconsin
>
> I was in executive sales with a Fortune 500 company, and my first reaction to MLM was negative. I was naive enough to think that I would make my money in the *work* world. In the work world I learned that my destiny was not in my control, but was controlled by the company for which I worked. I had a group of accounts, but they wouldn't let me expand my territory. Plus, they were not coming out with any new products.
>
> I began thinking. I asked myself if I was making what I was worth. I wondered, I had had so much fun working for myself when I was a kid, and then had grown up to be an employee of someone else! So, I decided to become the president of my own lemonade stand again.
>
> Another question came to my mind! How would you like to own your life—and make what you are worth?
>
> MLM is word-of-mouth advertising. With most business investments being so high, MLM is a reasonable way to get into business for yourself.

Now, do you *still* want to know *who sells* the product? A good analogy to the marketing of MLM products is the marketing of Hershey candy bars. Have you ever seen a Hershey candy bar store in your town? Probably not, but you *do* see a box or two of Hershey candy bars in most restaurants, convenience stores, drugstores, and a variety of other stores and businesses. You would probably never see any one location doing a tremendous amount of Hershey candy bar business; however, it still adds up to be a highly profitable and incredible success story!

You occasionally will see an MLM person who retails quite a lot of product, but that is the exception rather than the rule. Normally you will find, as with the Hershey candy bars, that most people in MLM will do a minimal amount of retailing. The large income in MLM is created when you add the downline volume to the total marketing plan. Marketing plans are based on all of the business that you and your downline organization create. This is another reason why it is so important to, like the athletic director, support and promote your down-line associates and their activities.

It is also important to keep or develop an open mind from the outset of your MLM career. Do not prejudge anyone who might benefit from your MLM opportunity.

For example, don't prejudge your dentist by automatically assuming that he would not be interested in an MLM opportunity. This is not only not being open minded, but nothing could be further from the truth since the dentist may well be interested. You never know until you ask. An important key here is to attempt to look at your opportunity from your prospect's perspective.

A doctor, dentist, or airline pilot, for instance, would not be able to perform their duties or further pursue their careers if something happened to their eyesight or if they lost the use of their hands. Most of them are very conscious of this fact, and for this reason most have investments or sideline businesses already working for them, thus making many of them excellent prospects for a good MLM opportunity.

Many professional people become very involved in multi-level marketing, working to multiply both their income and their security. By developing an open mind and looking at the positive aspects of MLM from other people's points of view, your sponsoring ratio and success will increase.

A physician once told me that multi-level marketing is very attractive to doctors, professionals, and other business people who have high overhead. This is because they desire additional income just like anyone else, but, as in the case of a physician, they are at a disadvantage. People in most occupations and/or careers do not earn income unless they personally are on the job. But their overhead continues even if they become ill and cannot be at the office.

Become aware that in many cases professional people are more open minded to MLM than the typical consumer. Keep in mind that middle- to upper-income professionals are normally more eager to consider and to evaluate new opportunities if only for the tax advantages that an MLM business offers them.

The achievements of thousands of networkers are helping

people to discover that the term "multi-level marketing" is synonymous with financial freedom, success, and people who are attaining better life styles.

A greater number of professional and business people are discovering that it is more fun to earn over $100,000 per year in MLM businesses than in the more conventional careers.

In MLM you are building a business similar to that of a real estate broker. You are recruiting other associates, but you don't have the expensive overhead of maintaining an office, phones, receptionists, secretaries, advertising, and so on.

Multi-level marketing can be as profitable, if not more profitable, as most franchise opportunities, but without the stress. An ever-increasing number of people who treat their MLM opportunity as a business instead of a hobby are developing incomes equal to most franchise owners. But there's a big difference—the life style and freedom that can be afforded by owning an MLM business.

The Smartest Way to Begin

Networking opportunities are limited only by one's own imagination. But for starters, let's check out a hypothetical scenario involving a new associate by the name of Harry to see how *he* started his MLM career.

Harry made an all-important decision in beginning his MLM business that immediately increased his odds of becoming successful. The smart decision that Harry made was to ask his sponsor, John, to assist him. Harry made an arrangement for John to come over to his house and help him make a few phone calls to set some recruiting appointments for the following Tuesday evening.

When John arrived, he instructed Harry on how to make his telephone calls. "Just ask your friends the following question," he said. "You're interested in making money, aren't you? With this approach, Harry, 98 percent of them will say yes. Invite them to get together at your house on Tuesday evening at 7:30 for approximately 45 minutes. Tell them you'd like them to meet me and to listen to a great way to make money. If they ask what it's all about, tell them *that* is what we are going to discuss when they get here. Tell them that there is no obligation and that we are simply going to share some exciting ideas with them and give them some literature and information to take home with them."

John relaxed Harry by saying, "Don't worry about the appointments you set, Harry, since I will be with you, and I'll do all the talking. You'll only have to observe, okay?"

Harry didn't feel that this would be too hard. After all, he didn't have to do anything but set appointments—John would make the entire presentation. Harry could sit back, let his friends come up with questions, and watch and listen as John answered them. Harry realized early on that asking for assistance was a smart thing to do. He decided to keep an open mind to learning important and invaluable basic concepts that could ensure his success in multi-level marketing.

Needless to say, Harry was motivated and excited with the support he was receiving from John. Within the hour, Harry had set up four appointments for Tuesday evening. Handling questions on the phone was not as difficult as Harry had originally thought because he had followed his sponsor's suggestions while putting forth a very positive attitude.

John, knowing the importance of recognition, congratulated Harry on what he had done. He told Harry that he had already accomplished more in his first hour in the business than many associates would do in a week. John asked Harry to show an opportunity videotape to several other friends and ask them to join them on Tuesday evening. He also instructed Harry to ask each of these people to bring a friend with them.

On Tuesday night, four out of the seven people Harry had invited were there, and two of them became associates! Harry was *really* excited! It had all been so simple—and fun!

Harry started off the evening by welcoming his guests into his home. He introduced John and asked his guests to listen with an open mind to what John had to say because the information had the potential to be very profitable for them.

With assurance, John showed the opportunity. There was no magic presentation, no high pressure—just a simple explanation that Harry would soon be able to do just as well as John had done. Harry had taken the attitude that if someone else could do this, he would copy them and eventually be able to do the same thing.

After the guests left, John asked Harry, "Would you like to discuss why this meeting went so well?" "Sure," Harry replied. John smiled and asked Harry to put a blank cassette in his tape recorder and to take some notes while he talked.

Beware that there are special approaches that work well with each MLM company; you must find the approach that works best for you. Also, you will normally have a better response from prospects when you state the name of your company or the nature of your product in your approach. By doing this, your prospects will be less skeptical and you can still pique their curiosity to listen to what you have to share.

Why We Joined MLM
Steve and Linda Rhodes, Vermont

Linda is a licensed practical nurse, and before my accident, I did carpentry work. Even though I get around in a wheelchair, there are days that I can't get out because of weather or illness. But my organization still makes sales, which means that *I* still make a profit!

What impressed me about multi-level marketing was the multiplication of numbers. At a certain point in the business, it can continue to grow on its own. I would encourage others in a situation similar to mine to do multi-level marketing. It's simple to do, can make you some good money, and it doesn't have to take up a lot of time.

There are days when I need extra rest or medical attention. If I were working for someone else, this could present a problem. With MLM, my income continues as my downline organization keeps growing.

Two Against One—A Definite Advantage

"One of the keys to recruiting this evening was simple," said John. "There were two of us. All we had to do was to convince one of the people here tonight to our way of thinking. And our way of thinking *must* have some merit, because there are already two of us who believe it!" John continued, "It is a lot easier for a prospect to catch our enthusiasm than it is for him to convince both of us that we're wrong. Remember what you have seen here tonight, Harry. New associates will do much better when they have someone working with them."

As you reread this story you can pick up several good tips. There is an excellent example of the sponsor assisting a new associate. Of course, every meeting does not culminate with new prospects joining your business. The point is that by being consistent in assisting your downline, you will have many good meetings along with those that are not so good. By using the successful ideas you learn from your upline leaders, you will increase the percentage of your good meetings.

Let's shift gears and see how networking worked for two fund-raising projects.

A successful Oklahoma businessman shared with me how he served as chairman and donated his time and ideas to help two churches meet their goals of completing building projects while remaining debt-free (see chart, page 27).

The chairman's first experience in fund raising through networking involved approximately 1,000 adults attending Sunday school at the church, which ultimately raised more than $3.5 million. His second attempt involved approximately 180 adults attending Sunday school at a second church, and raised over $1.5 million. Since their goal was identical, both churches used the theme "Together We Build." Both programs followed the same network structure to raise their money.

First there were four weeks of organizing the network fund-raising project. Everything was done with the full approval of the church pastor. The pastor and the chairman established the need. Because of his busy schedule, the chairman appointed two assistants to carry through with small yet important details, such as paperwork, phone calls, and double-checking lists and figures. A book was developed and produced that told the history of the church, listed current events, and included a church directory.

Why We Joined MLM
Hason and Rabiah Bakr, New York

My husband is a musician, and I worked as a software systems design analyst when we got involved in multi-level marketing. To us, multi-level marketing is like having distribution points all over the country with no overhead. It is an awesome concept. We live in New York, but we have people in Hawaii adding to our income!

We are very happy with multi-level marketing now, but we had sworn off it for a while, which was a big mistake! At first we found it difficult to find a company that was solid and suitable to us, but we've learned that a few bad companies don't make the whole industry bad.

There is no cap on the possibilities of income in multi-level marketing. We are doing very well and are setting our goals to what we want to have.

Five key church leaders were chosen. This was the most important aspect of the project, as you will see, so these five people needed to be very committed to the future of the church.

The pastor made the initial financial contribution to the fund. Except for meetings with the chairman to keep him updated, the pastor had no other involvement in the raising of the money.

The chairman personally talked with both assistants and each of his five key leaders regarding their personal donations. Some of the donations were made in cash or property, and other donations were made in the form of pledges that did not exceed two years. The church pledged 2 percent of the normal Sunday donations for two years. All of the donations and pledges to date were totaled and applied toward the final goal.

The five key leaders began building their networks by finding five people each, for a total involvement of an additional 25 people. These 30 people personally invited others to their homes, and those attending these in-home meetings were given a copy of the church book. In addition, a presentation consisting of a brief history of the church and information regarding the current building project was given.

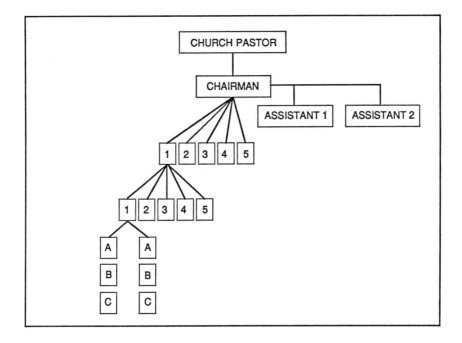

Church Fund-Raising Network Structure

The amount of donations and pledges to date was announced at these meetings. Those people who had made the donations gave public testimonies, although no individual dollar amounts were discussed.

At the end of the four weeks, a network of supporters had been developed. Then there was a two-day blitz whereby all of the church members were contacted.

Public testimonies were given at the Sunday services to kick off the two-day blitz. Each of the five key leaders met each of his five supporters. Each leader discussed a preorganized list of names with the supporters he was working with.

The objective of this meeting was to assist the supporters in finding two donors each and to, in turn, help each of those donors to find one more person each. Totals were tallied and announced at a special dinner banquet to which all the church members and their friends were invited. Through a form of networking, inspired by multi-level marketing, each church building project goal was achieved. They had raised the necessary funds to complete their individual building projects, and they remained debt free!

Duplicate Yourself

You've now read about the MLM freedom and life style. Is this just a lot of hype—a fantasy—or can it become a reality? Think about reality!

A franchise opportunity does not just build itself. A franchise owner needs to commit the time necessary to make the franchise successful. The same is true with any good MLM opportunity. You need to commit yourself to working it as you would any other business. But, once you have *made* that commitment, the MLM freedom and life style *can* become a reality. Assuming that you are going to commit time and energy to your MLM business instead of a conventional business opportunity, why is it more possible to have this freedom with multi-level marketing?

The answer is simple. So simple that many people miss it. Duplication. That's it—the duplication of your efforts. Each of you who learns to duplicate yourself by developing other people in your downline organization into leaders will find that MLM can provide you with not only the large income you are looking for, but also the time to enjoy the benefits of that large income. The key words here are *for each of you who learn to duplicate yourself by developing other people into leaders*.

Financial freedom will not come to those of you who do not ask questions, who do not commit the time, who do not follow through with their new downline, and who do not *learn to duplicate* themselves. It *will be attained by doing all of these things*—but most importantly by learning to duplicate your efforts!

MLM Success Profile:
The Clayton and Charlotte Overton Story

Clayton Overton is an orthopedic surgeon who is involved in many community activities, such as serving on the hospital board and the school board. At one time Charlotte taught school, but now she assists her husband with their Amway business and in raising their children.

"I saw the MLM opportunity with Amway about the time that malpractice insurance rates in California went from $7,000 to $25,000 per year," says Clayton. My first impression of multi-level marketing was that this could be a form of diversification to offset the cost of the malpractice insurance."

Charlotte adds, "At first I didn't see the large income potential that the business had to offer. I don't like to entertain the thought of what would happen to us as a family if something happened to Clayton, but now we would be able to maintain our life style as a family."

"I usually work 60 to 80 hours a week in my medical practice, but my company's MLM program gives me the opportunity to cut out my night calls and cut my practice down to three days a week whenever I choose," continues Clayton. "I never want to get out of medicine, because I love it too much. Still, I want time with my family. We are now able to travel and vacation together more, and have a more personal life style. The additional freedom is great!

"We set a goal to match our six-figure medical income with the MLM program in five or six years. We reached that in just three years," says Clayton.

"And we've had travel experiences that are beyond our wildest dreams. We were on a picture African safari tour with the renowned John Goddard," Charlotte continued. "We've been to Hawaii, to Hong Kong, on cruises in the Caribbean islands, and to Alaska on a private yacht cruise. One of our children experienced a world tour, and the other spent his junior year in college studying abroad and traveling throughout Europe."

"It's nice to have the option to retire early from medicine if I ever elect to," Clayton asserts. "What most professional people don't realize about multi-level marketing is that if you put in five good years working at it, it can take care of you for life. Yet in medicine I put four years into medical school and one year in internship plus orthopedic training, which gives me the opportunity to work 60 to 80 hours a week the rest of my life!

"Another thing I like about multi-level marketing is that, like most professional people, I've made some investments. Someone else usually had total control of my money, and, in some cases, had lost it. With the MLM system, I have total control of my downline business. It takes a minimum investment, there's no financial risk, and the hours are flexible—and that is *very* important to my medical practice," Clayton says.

"With an MLM business, the income continues to come in and there is no overhead. In medicine I get paid by the hour for the time that I work. As long as I'm working, I make a very good income. But when I quit working, that money stops, but the tremendous overhead continues. If you are a professional person, get over any image problems that you may have, and just do the business!

"We've made a lot of friendships in this business," continues Charlotte. "And people are grateful when you help them become successful. We are able to do things now that we were never able to do before. Now we have help in the house and yard because we are not tied to a budget as we were when we just had Clayton's practice. We now have dreams that we would never have had before. We even bought a vacation home on St. John's Island in the Caribbean."

"Because of duplication," concludes Clayton, "MLM gives me freedom."

Clayton and Charlotte's Keys to Success

Income diversification today is a way of life. Most corporations have recognized that income diversification is necessary in order to keep their corporate profits up and to overcome trends and changes in the marketplace.

Multiple incomes are the wave of the future. Most of us as individuals are going to have to develop other income sources to achieve luxury and any real security that we might want in our lives.

Time becomes a very ordinary, common excuse for many people, but if someone *really* wants to do something, he or she will find the time to do it. The beautiful thing is that, because of duplication, a little bit of time invested in a good MLM program can be leveraged and multiplied into a lot of productive time. In other words, when you have an organization with hundreds of people with a *little* bit of time, the sum total adds up to a *whole lot* of time! This is the whole marketing strategy with MLM.

The only people who don't have time are those in the obituary column. *Their* time is up. You and I have a lot of time left, and so it's not a matter of *having* time, but of rearranging priorities.

Chapter
3

YOUR FIRST 90 DAYS: BEGINNING TIPS

The first and most important step in beginning your MLM business is to simply start. It is also the most difficult step to take, because we tend to make excuses for the fears we have. Strangely enough though, action cures fear. W. Clement Stone popularized a statement to help overcome fear and procrastination: *"Do it now!"*

It is important to begin your business with a sense of urgency. Fire, ready, aim is the order of the day. Start immediately! Then organize your downline associates as your business grows. Do not worry about how you will handle the organization you intend to build. You bring the people in, and, *if you ask for help*, some upline leaders will assist you in stabilizing your business.

Before we get to our Beginning Tips, let's first talk about fear. It is natural to experience certain fears when beginning a new project. The most common fear is probably that of failure. It is important to realize that most people feel fear to some degree. What is even more important is that you do not take it personally.

Let's analyze some of the most basic fears that new associates have, and look at some solutions:

1. The fear that your prospect will not be interested.
   Solution: Realize that it's a numbers game. Many people will be interested in your opportunity; however, a number of people will not be. When dealing with those who are not interested, simply ask for a referral. Chances are that they will know someone who *will* be interested.
2. The fear of what others will think.
   Solution: No matter what you do or do not do, there

will always be those who wish you well and those who do not. Ask yourself these very simple questions, "Is the company I am with reputable? Does this company offer an excellent value in its products and/or services?" If the answer is yes, then be proud of your company, be proud of yourself, and go for it!

3. The fear that you do not have enough time to do a good job.
   Solution: One of the many strengths of multi-level marketing is that there is help if you will only ask for it. Also, there is the magic of duplicating your efforts through sponsoring others. In fact, if you are extremely busy, you will be forced by your personal lack of time to delegate leadership to other people. Incidentally, "lack of time" is a poor excuse. It is just a matter of setting priorities and balancing one's time.

4. The fear that you won't be able to answer the questions that your prospects will have.
   Solution: Simply say, "Let me write down your questions, and I will call you with an answer tomorrow." Then be sure to do it.

Success is not reserved for the most talented. It is there for those who *go after it*. Over 100 years ago Abraham Lincoln said, "Things may come to those who wait, but only those things left over by those who hustle!" Think about this statement! Let it make a lasting impression on you.

Now that you are determined to start now, here are some practical tips that will help to get you off to a better start:

1. *Make a list of names immediately.* (See chart, page 36) Do not prejudge anyone! Continually add to this list as more people come to mind. Use your Christmas card list. Write down the names of the people that you know who have previously been in a multi-level business. And, besides yourself, who is the most ambitious person that you know? Do not exclude relatives. Look at it this way—someone is going to contact them sooner or later, why shouldn't it be you? Realize that the names you place on this list can be worth over $1 million to you.

WHO DO YOU KNOW?

1. Who is ambitious?   _____
2. Who has teenagers?   _____
3. Who owns their own business?   _____
4. Who is a salesperson?   _____
5. Who has investments?   _____
6. Who do people seem to like?   _____
7. Who works for you?   _____
8. Who lives in your neighbor-
   hood?   _____
9. Who are relatives?   _____
10. Who shared an opportunity with
    you?   _____
11. Who sells real estate?   _____
12. Who is retired?   _____
13. Who is in direct sales?   _____
14. Who is a working woman?   _____
15. Who is a teacher?   _____
16. Who is a single parent?   _____
17. Who prepares tax returns?   _____
18. Who is a retired military officer?   _____
19. Who is out of work?   _____
20. Who recently bought a new
    house?   _____

2. *Set up a meeting in your or a friend's home.* Keep every aspect of the meeting as simple as possible.

a. Start on time. Seven-thirty seems to be a good meeting time.

b. End on time. This type of opportunity meeting should not normally last longer than 45 minutes to an hour.

c. Ask your sponsor, an upline leader, or another associate to assist you with your first few meetings. Later, you'll feel more comfortable putting them on yourself.

d. Read Chapter 6, "How to Hold Meetings," for other details.

e. *Have fun!*

3. *See people one-on-one.*

a. Be spontaneous! Ask everyone you come in contact with that all-important question: "You like to make money, don't you?" If you don't already have it, develop the you-never-know-until-you-ask attitude.

b. Use leverage. If you were going to move a refrigerator across your kitchen, you would use leverage by using a two-wheeler or a dolly to help push this heavy object, wouldn't you? You are interested in "moving people" into your business. Instead of physical leverage, you can have mental and emotional assistance by lending your prospects a cassette or videotape.

c. Sponsor both personally and downline. Personal sponsoring is when you have signed up an associate directly under you. Downline sponsoring happens when you work with your new personally-sponsored associate and the two of you together talk with his friends. Those that are signed up by your associate will still benefit you because they become a person in your downline. And *don't procrastinate!* Work with your associates and see their prospects. They are more likely to get off to a great start and keep their natural enthusiasm with your help. Besides, it's fun working together!

4. *Use the telephone.*

a. Realize that the purpose of your phone call is not to get people interested in your business opportunity. The purpose of your phone call is to simply set an appointment to *show* your business opportunity.

b. Remember to smile when you talk on the phone. Telephone operators are taught to smile when they talk on the phone, so why shouldn't you smile, too? You will be more enthusiastic when you do—and more importantly, you will *sound* more enthusiastic.

c. Clear the negatives out of your mind before you call anyone. Everyone has an occasional bad day. Don't let it affect you in a negative way. The MLM opportunity you are involved with can bring you financial freedom. This makes it important to give it your best shot.

d. Keep your phone calls short and to the point. Your phone approach might go something like this?

YOU   "Jane, are you going to be home this evening?"

JANE   "Yes."

YOU   "You wouldn't mind my stopping by for a moment and leaving you a cassette tape that I think you would like to hear, would you?"

JANE   "What's it all about?"

YOU   "The cassette tape will explain the details of an interesting new project and way to make money, Jane. You know, this may not be for you, but it's worth looking at, and there's no obligation. How about 6:00 p.m., or would 6:30 be better?"

Use a tone of voice that shows you expect your prospect to allow you to stop by for a moment. Stay relaxed and have fun! Not everyone will see you, but with this type of approach, many will.

Here is the same basic approach with just a little different wording. Take these ideas and develop an approach that works for you. Remember to keep it simple!

YOU   "Sam, you like to save money, don't you?"

SAM   "Yes, of course."

YOU   "I've come across something that really looks good and would like to drop off some information for you to look at. What's good for you, tomorrow evening, or would you mind if I stopped by briefly tonight?"

SAM   "How long will this take?"

YOU   "Just 20 to 25 minutes. This may not be for you, Sam, but it doesn't hurt to take a look. What's better for you, tomorrow or this evening?"

Both of these introductions get right to the point in a re-spectful and friendly, but businesslike atmosphere. As you de-velop your own approach, remember to word it to *get an ap-pointment*, not to promote interest.

Relax your prospect to encourage him or her to take a look at your business—this is your objective! Don't try to sell him or her on the telephone. Let the cassette or videotape you are dropping off do the work for you—remember, *leverage*! The tapes are a leverage tool working for you.

Another important technique used here is an attempt to see your prospect the same evening you are calling. To do this, offer the later alternative first, then "this evening" second. This relaxes your prospect, and he or she is more likely to see you that same evening.

You may want to offer a time to drop off the tape on your way to a 7:30 meeting. This will make your time much more productive. And who knows—when your prospect finds out where you're going, maybe he or she will want to go with you.

Conference-Call Recruiting

Another excellent Beginning Tip involves the use of the three-way conference-call feature, which is available on most phone systems today.

Picture this. You have just sponsored a new associate, Joe Smith. You have asked him to make a list of people that he knows, and you've reviewed his list with him. Now you'll call Joe and the first prospect on his list from your telephone. When the prospect answers the call, Joe will speak first and greet his friend. He will then immediately introduce you so that Joe's friend will know that you are also on the phone.

Joe will then briefly explain to his friend that he is looking at an excellent opportunity and that he is calling because he "needs some help." This is where you take over by mentioning that you and Joe are working together and would like to briefly discuss your business with him to see if he would possibly be able to refer you to some people who might be interested in it.

Why I Joined MLM
John Sungail, Florida

I have always been happy and secure in my full-time career as a manufacturer's representative working with a capital equipment manufacturer in the plastic and printing industry. I also have numerous property and rental investments.

The duplication process originally attracted me to the MLM industry. You only have 24 hours in a day, and you can only be in one place at any one time. But with multi-level marketing you can clone yourself to multiply your income.

There are no employer–employee relationships in multi-level marketing. You are in business *for yourself,* but not *by yourself.* MLM can easily be worked successfully along with a full-time profession.

Ask if you can talk with him for a few minutes. Ordinarily he will say yes. If he is busy, ask if you and Joe can call him back later, or ask if Joe can drop off a cassette or videotape for him to listen to. Normally you will be able to talk to most people at the time of your call.

Proceed by briefly explaining what your feature product or service is. Also mention that you have a marketing program and are looking for a few people who like to make money.

Ask the person you are talking with whom he knows that you and Joe could call or who would be interested in listening to a tape that would explain the opportunity.

Keep this phone call casual; don't make it educational. Use a persuasive tone of voice, but not hyped up or pushy. Above all, be respectful. After all, these are Joe's friends.

If any of the prospects are not responsive at any time during the phone call, be polite, thank them for their time, hang up, and phone the next person on the list.

Your objective is not to receive a referral from each of the people you call, nor is it to get each of them interested in your business. Your objective is to *reach a percentage* of those you call. As you better understand what your objective is—to reach a percentage rather than every prospect—the percentage of people who become interested will actually increase.

You will be able to contact at least five or more prospects each evening with Joe by following this "conference-call" method of recruiting. When done correctly, this can be a very effective way of rapidly expanding your business.

This is a method that can work at any time. All it takes is a desire to build your business and a three-way conference-call telephone system from your local phone company. If neither you nor your associate has a three-way phone system, go over to your associate's house and get on one of his or her extension phones. It's the same principle—you can both talk at the same time to your prospects.

When you use the conference-call method, you greatly multiply the number of people you can reach. Make time to stop at someone's home on your way to a 7:30 p.m. meeting and make three to five phone calls with that associate. This is a simple suggestion that will make a big difference to your profitability.

And since one of the most important assets of multi-level marketing is the ability to duplicate oneself, find associates in your downline who will follow this simple system.

If you are new to an MLM opportunity, call an upline leader to assist you in getting started. Don't be afraid to ask for help.

Here are some other key tips that will assist you:

1. *Let your excitement show.* Don't be afraid to show your feelings. Human nature is to be somewhat reserved or withdrawn so that we can't be hurt, but in doing this, we can also *become* reserved and mask our joy and excitement for what we are doing.

2. *Watch your prospects' eyes.* This will tell you whether or not they are listening to you. It is important for you to "read between the lines" when you are talking with your prospects to see whether they are truly sincere in their interest.

3. *Sell the sizzle.* People will ask you detailed questions if you get too detailed with your presentation, and in doing so they will probably miss the point. When you stay with highlights, your prospects will more likely see a way for their dreams to come true.

Nothing happens unless first a dream.
                                          Carl Sandburg

4. *Involve your prospects immediately.* Develop the habit of asking your prospects to write down the names of people they would like to have look at the business as you finish sharing the opportunity. When you do this, the percentage of people that you sponsor will go up dramatically because you are involving them with you right at the beginning. Also, as they write the names down, they will begin to visualize others becoming involved with them.

5. *Use the test-market approach.* Sometimes your prospects will not be sure whether they want to get started in your business at a particular time. Should this happen, simply say, "Let's test market this opportunity with several of your friends to get their reactions."

Successful fast-food restaurants will test market new food items in a particular area before adding them to their menus nationwide. If the test market works out, they will offer that item throughout the country. On the other hand, if the item does not do well, they will drop it. Relate a story like this to your prospects when you suggest that they test market your business. It makes sense, and it will make sense to many of your prospects.

You have everything to gain and nothing to lose by using this approach. You will want to test market the business with at least four or five of your prospect's friends. When any one of the friends decides to join, your prospect will automatically join.

Consider this: You were just hired to coach a major college football or basketball team. You would be excited and challenged with the opportunity to build a winning team, wouldn't you? You need to motivate your team to have that desire to win big. You need to teach fair play and fundamentals, and encourage extra effort. Along with organizing a system of plays, you will also need to be aware of good public relations.

Each of these areas is important. Of course, many of these functions will be delegated, but as head coach, *you* are ultimately responsible.

There is one function, though, that is more important than all of these others combined. To win big, you need to be an excellent recruiter. Recruiting top-notch assistant coaches and players is a numbers game; you will interview many athletes before finding the few who will join the team.

Multi-level marketing is much the same. Your most important job is to recruit people and find those who have a desire to do something special with their lives. One of the great strengths of multi-level marketing is that the people you personally sponsor will in turn sponsor people they know. Because of this, your chances of becoming successful through networking versus other opportunities multiplies. And you can have a number of committed key people sponsored in your downline organization who will add greatly to your income.

Think Small to Grow Big

Now let's look realistically at the new people joining your organization. Many new people who join downline organizations do not get off to a quick start because of procrastination. And many people will procrastinate regardless of what they are doing. All these people need is a helping hand, just a nudge in the right direction. The largest and most successful networkers are very good at working with new people, and it's really a very simple process. Realize this, and you will find that the easiest way to sponsor new associates is by helping others to see their friends and by going with them to drop off cassette and videotapes at their friends' homes.

This leads to the principle of "thinking small to grow big" in your MLM business. Let me explain. New networkers often try to personally sponsor as many people as they can. This is much like throwing mud against a wall and seeing how much will stick. When you personally sponsor new associates, take time to work with them to help them begin to establish their downline organizations. If you are doing a good job of assisting your new associates, you will end up sponsoring a smaller number of new associates personally, but you will ultimately end up with a bigger and more profitable organization.

As you recruit your new associates, allow them to participate with you in meetings. They may assist you initially by
doing the introduction to the meeting, or they may talk briefly
on a related subject during some portion of the meeting. Later,
as their confidence grows, let them do a part of the meeting
presentation, such as the product demonstration or the opportunity itself.

Why We Joined MLM
Chuck and Jewel Rodgers, Georgia

During my final year in the Navy, I began looking for
things to do. Even though I would retire on a commander's
pension, three of our four children were still in college. We
looked at franchises. Most jobs we looked at were like
jumping out the frying pan and into the fire! After 28 years
with Navy, we were ready for *more* freedom in our lives
than a job would offer, not *less!*

My first perception of multi-level marketing was that
it was a door-to-door business. As we got home from our
first meeting, though, we kept discussing the quality of the
people there. People from all walks of life—including airline pilots, a doctor, a veterinarian, and a preacher, among
other professionals and nonprofessionals—had been
there. So we went back for a second look to see what we
had missed the first time around, and we found a strong
opportunity.

We started before retirement. We realized that an
MLM business wouldn't grow unless we worked at it. At
one of the meetings we heard the statement, "gold in the
pockets is inversely proportional to lead in the britches."
Multi-level marketing has given Jewell and me a common
ground to enable us to work together. It has helped us stay
younger, because we are continually working with younger people. We look at our MLM business as an ever-ex-
panding family.

Step by step, they will grow in self-confidence and take
over the leadership of their own businesses, which will in turn
benefit yours. This method of working with your people helps
them to build a solid foundation upon which a much bigger
business can be built. This philosophy emphasizes the impor-

tance of first learning and then doing the basics instead of just trying to hit home runs without any training.

Most people would like to do well and would probably do better if they just had someone to assist them at the beginning. Assistance is a two-way phone call—you calling your downline to assist them but also calling your upline leader when *you* need some support. Many times there is someone in your upline who is willing to help, but they won't know you need help unless you ask.

The Oyster Parable

Suppose that you are a professional pearl hunter sitting on a dock by the sea. Every hour you are given a bucket of 100 oysters. Among the 100 oysters are five that have pearls. The other 95 are empty. You take out the first oyster, cut it open, and find it empty. Would you then carefully put it back together, hold it between your hands to keep it warm, and then sit there for days hoping it would grow a pearl? Of course not! You would throw the empty oyster away and reach for more and more oysters until you have found the ones with the pearls!

Unfortunately, many new beginning associates treat their friends and new prospects like the empty oyster. Instead of simply going on to another new prospect, they keep hoping, asking, inviting, and pleading with the same people week after week. Some of these associates never understand that they need to break the habit of working too long with empty oysters.

One of the Keys to Recruiting Is Not *Convincing* People, But *Sorting* People

You can burn yourself out and become discouraged trying to work with people who just don't have enough desire and drive to realize their dreams. Your job as a professional MLM recruiter is to sort through the prospects until you find one who wants to become an associate, then proceed to discover who will become the active associates and who will become the inactive ones.

It Is Easier to Give Birth Than to Resurrect the Dead

It is much easier to find a new prospect who wants to work than to convince an unmotivated, uninterested, or inactive person to work.

How to Handle Advertising

Normally, short ads placed in the Help Wanted section of the newspaper work best. Some MLM companies restrict the use of their name in ads, so you would run what are called "blind ads." Blind ads are generic ads that do not mention anything about the company you represent. Here are two examples of blind ads:

A SALESPERSON'S DREAM

National company offering new service everyone needs & can afford. No competition. Part & full time. Call 555-2020.

I am looking for 8 *good people* to work with me on a PART or FULL TIME basis to earn some serious money. Call J. B. Smith, 555-2020.

As in any business, it is important that you shop and compare to find where you will get the best return for your advertising dollar. Ads can be relatively inexpensive. Instead of running an ad in your local paper for 30 consecutive days, for example, run it over a period of six months to one year by taking advantage of the special three-day rate once a month. Ask the person who takes your ad at the newspaper to read it back to you to make sure there are no mistakes. Also ask how many words you would need to eliminate to get a lower rate. You can sometimes drop as few as one or two words and be able to save several dollars per day in expenses.

Where to Place Your Ads

1. *Local Daily newspapers.* Good circulation, but usually more expensive than other types of newspapers.

2. *Weekly newspapers.* Less circulation than a daily newspaper, but usually less expensive, and you have less competition with other ads.

3. *Free shoppers' papers.* These are normally distributed locally on a weekly basis. Available at restaurants, convenience stores, and other high-traffic areas. Inexpensive advertising, and the ad section is read by an extremely high percentage of people.

4. *Magazines, national newspapers, radio, and television.* Very expensive, but reach a large market. You must be experienced enough to follow through with leads, since many of them will come from out of town.

What do ads give you? Leads! Don't have the misconception that ads will give you new associates—they won't. You should not expect to sponsor a lot of people from the ads you place. Instead, you will receive a number of calls from curious people. Work to achieve two objectives from these calls:

1. To sponsor at least one, or perhaps two or three associates.
2. To ask for referrals from the people who respond to your ad but show no interest in your opportunity.

Many very successful MLM stars first got involved in multi-level marketing through answering an ad. Some were at points in their lives where they were looking for a better opportunity. In other cases, they were just curious. Either way, they responded to an ad. And if it had been yours, as an upline leader, you would have benefited greatly from their success.

The following might be a typical response when people call about your ad:

CALLER   I'm calling about your ad.

YOU   Fine, my name is [your name], what is your name, please?
(Write down the person's name . . . and then use it!)

CALLER   Joe Smith.

YOU   Joe, I'm glad you called. The name of our com-
          pany is [name of your company]. Our home
          office is located in [city and state]. Have you
          ever heard of us?/You've heard of us, haven't
          you?

CALLER   Yes/No.

YOU   By the way, Joe, I'm receiving a lot of phone
          calls. In case we're cut off here, what's your
          phone number?

CALLER   555-2020

YOU   Joe, our company was founded in [year]. We
          have over [number] in assets and provide a ser-
          vice/product that everyone needs and cannot
          afford to be without. (At this point, make a few
          personal comments about your product or op-
          portunity. Once you have done this, finish
          with a leading question). Joe, you can see that
          this is a product that would be of interest to a
          lot of people, can't you?

CALLER   Yes.

YOU   Joe, let me ask you, What kind of work are you
          doing now? Have you had any sales or man-
          agement experience? How long have you lived
          in this area? Does your wife work? (Select a few
          of these questions to ask in a relaxed manner.
          These questions will help you to become more
          familiar with your prospects.) Joe, I'd like to
          meet with you. Could you meet with me to-
          morrow morning, or would this afternoon be
          better?

At this point, the caller may begin to ask questions. This is
fine, as long as you keep control by giving short answers. Then
again attempt to schedule the appointment to meet by offering
a choice of two times. For example:

CALLER   Can you send me some literature?

YOU   Yes, Joe, I could, but I never send literature
          unless I can meet with you for just ten or 15

minutes so that I can briefly go over what we have. Then I'd be glad to leave all the literature you want plus a cassette tape to listen to. What is the best time for you to meet with me, tomorrow morning or this afternoon?

CALLER I want to know more about this before I meet with you and make a decision.

YOU I agree with you, Joe, because I feel much the same way. Joe, my attitude is that, if we *do* meet, it's not because you're interested in our business, but that you're just curious to get some details so that you can make a decision later. You would want to meet with me personally before you make any decisions anyway, and, of course, I would want to meet with you so that I could decide whether I want to work with you or not. So which is a better time for us to get together, tomorrow morning or this afternoon?

Why I Joined MLM
Carol Leuffgen, Michigan

As a housewife and mother, I wanted to help supplement our family income, but I didn't want to leave my children with babysitters. When I first heard about multi-level marketing, the idea sounded great to me because I saw that I could earn good money in my spare time. And I could set my own hours to work around my family's schedule!

I think multi-level marketing is great! I don't look at it as selling, but as working with people. Most of the people I recruit are everyday people. They are people who are tired of staying where they are and have a desire to grow in life.

Working hard in multi-level marketing is just showing the products and telling a story. I believe in what I'm doing, and I never have a boring day!

As you can see, the technique here is to give a short answer, and then attempt to set the appointment. Furthermore, the whole approach to people who call about your ad should be a very relaxed one. Always give your caller a small amount of information before you ask him or her for information. This give–ask formula is very relaxing and effective.

There is no hard and fast rule on where to meet with people; it depends on the individual situation. You will develop a knack for screening prospects by the answers they give to the few questions you ask them. You will be able to determine their level of determination and ambition, and this will help you to decide where to meet with your prospects. Restaurants are very desirable meeting places, and can enable you to meet with two separate prospects at the same time. You will also want to invite your prospects to your weekly meeting.

Hopefully you will be receiving a number of phone calls. Because it is difficult to see everyone, you must set some guidelines to help you spend your time wisely. There are two important things to remember here: do not attempt to prejudge anyone, and, of course, if they are not interested, always ask for referrals.

MLM Success Profile: The Anne Newbury Story

Anne Newbury is a graduate of the University of Texas who currently resides with her husband and four children in Massachusetts.

"My first real exposure to an MLM-type concept," Anne relates, "was when I was visiting my parents in Dallas. I was having dinner with a cousin whose husband was in the real-estate business. He asked me if I had ever considered going into business for myself and began telling me about Mary Kay Cosmetics. At first I prejudged it as a door-to-door business, but, because he was so impressed with the company and their marketing plan, I decided to check into it. I contacted a friend of theirs," Anne continues, "and asked her to send me some literature. She wisely invited me to lunch!

"After talking with her, I was also impressed, and I decided to give it a try. 'Nothing ventured, nothing gained,' I thought. I felt that I owed it to myself to try a new venture.

"It wasn't always easy, and I considered quitting on more than one occasion. But when I was expecting my third child," she says, "I realized that there would be a real need for more income. I had already seen what I could do on a part-time basis, and I decided to see what I could do if I did it more seriously.

"Since 1973 I have earned a new Cadillac every year. I've also won many beautiful pieces of jewelry, among them a diamond watch, a diamond bracelet, and diamond necklaces. The things I've worked for the hardest, however, were the Top Ten trips. I've been fortunate enough to travel first class all over the world. I have been to Europe, Hong Kong, Thailand, Australia, the Greek isles, and Israel. These were fabulous trips that I would not have been able to send myself on.

"My income the first year as a director was about $5,000," she continues, "but now my annual income is nearly a quarter of a million dollars. I am a member of Mary Kay's Millionaire Club, which means that I've passed the million-dollar mark in earnings. I am now better than two-thirds of the way toward my second million in just the past three years.

"With this marketing plan, I've seen women from all walks of life do well not only financially, but also in personal growth.

"Positive thinking has done wonders for my life. I believe that you can do anything that you put your heart, mind, and soul into. I also believe that work is the best therapy in the world," Anne concludes.

Anne's Key to Success

I learned early on how important it is to plan my time in order to be both efficient and effective. Being a homemaker with a busy household, I found it imperative to get up at least an hour earlier than I ever had before. I had to realize that Rome wasn't built in a day! But work every single day, and, with the marketing plan, your goal will inevitably be realized.

I have learned how infectious enthusiasm is, and what it can do to affect your family as well as your sales career. People are drawn to enthusiasm.

My determination is strong. I try to fulfill every goal that I set, but it takes perseverance.

Being able to see the potential in other people is a key factor. I love to visualize what other people can become and what they can have if they are willing to pay the price.

A big benefit in working with people in this business is that you learn how to live by the Golden Rule. This includes learning not to criticize other people, learning not to judge people without first having walked in their shoes, and learning to sandwich any constructive criticism between tons of praise. In other words, treat others the way you want to be treated. Somehow it always comes back to you the way that it is supposed to.

It's important to learn to be an optimist. People will either find a way to get what they want or they will find an excuse not to. Procrastination is our own worst enemy.

Go to work! I truly believe that whatever the mind can conceive and believe in, *can*, in fact, be achieved. Setting a good example is another primary key to success. *You* may be the only gospel that some people will *ever* get to read!

Chapter
4

MLM PRINCIPLES THAT GET RESULTS

If you owned a manufacturing facility, wouldn't you want to operate it as efficiently as possible? Sure you would! Time is money, and you would wish for your investment to pay off well.

Why shouldn't you approach your MLM business with the same attitude? Why not be profitable? As simple as this statement sounds, many people are *hoping* something will happen instead of attempting to *make* something happen.

There are three kinds of people in this world:

1. Those who *hope* for things to happen
2. Those who *wonder* what is happening
3. Those who *make* things happen

At some point in their careers, network leaders, people like you and me, had to begin thinking like leaders. You become what you think about, and there are basic principles that work for network leaders that can work just as well for you. As you read these principles, be determined to copy and rework them to fit your personality.

The Spare-Tire Principle

When you drive a car, you carry a spare tire, right? Why? Are you negative? Do you expect to have a flat tire? Of course, not! You carry a spare tire just in case you have a flat, don't you? Well this principle can be applied to this business.

When you work out of town with an associate, try to sponsor another associate for yourself at the same time. This second associate, in essence, becomes your spare tire in case the first associate "goes flat." If *both* groups do well, then you have doubled your profits. Go the extra mile by sponsoring the second associate. Consistent extra effort pays off in the long run.

You are probably thinking about just how obvious this principle is, but you would be amazed at how few people really apply it. Probably fewer than 20 percent! This coincides with the 80/20 rule, which states that 80 percent of the business is done by 20 percent of the people. So, very simply, if you wish to be one of the top 20 percent, apply the Spare-Tire Principle!

The Ten-Balloon Principle

Let's pretend for a moment that we are playing darts. Put one balloon on the board, and throw a dart at it. With one balloon on the dart board, what are your chances of breaking it? You may or may not hit the balloon, right?

Now put ten balloons on the board and throw a dart at them. With ten balloons to throw at you are more likely to be successful in hitting at least one balloon.

The one balloon we hit in this illustration represents a leader. This business is a numbers game. When you are working with a new associate, you are more likely to find an excited person downline who will develop into a leader when you see at least ten prospects.

There are several ways to increase the number of prospects you contact so that you can see ten or more:

1. Organize one or more in-home seminars.
2. Place an ad in the help-wanted section of your local newspaper.
3. Ride with your new associate for in-person visits with his or her friends.
4. Ask your new associate to purchase ten opportunity cassette tapes to lend to his or her friends.
5. Ask your new associate to purchase at least one videotape for showing.

The 3–30–300 Principle

As you begin to sponsor and work downline, the associates in your organization will take all of your time if you let them. It doesn't matter whether you have three, 30, 300, or 3,000.

Why we Joined MLM
Jim and Ann Cue, Wisconsin

Jim was a painting contractor, and I taught high school and college English. The key thing that we saw in MLM initially was duplication—with this business we were able to duplicate our efforts, which gave us the satisfaction of seeing many more lives touched for the better. It also gave us the financial freedom to allow us to upgrade the quality of our lives.

It took us a while to get our MLM program going. We started doing well when we stopped letting ourselves get sidetracked, made a commitment to our company, and taught the program. Also, we had to learn to run multilevel marketing as a business, and we work hard to encourage positive thinking.

We have been experts at survival, and now we are becoming experts at living. After one and a half years with our present company, we are averaging over $7,500 per month income. We have found we can do a lot more good in this world *with* money than without it. We are very happy with our choice of company and with the MLM field.

The point is that you need to learn to delegate and continue to sponsor new associates, thus adding to your organization until your goals have been achieved. You cannot be everything to everyone. You will need to make decisions on where it is best to invest your time.

As your organization grows, your priorities with respect to time will change. In the beginning, for example, you will spend more time personally sponsoring new associates and involving yourself in retail sales projects to generate your business volume. As you grow, however, you will find people to whom you will be able to delegate a lot of leadership. In other words, where once you were the leader of the organization, you ultimately take a supportive role and assist those you have become your key people—those who have grown to take over the leadership of their own organizations. By building others up as leaders of their own organizations, you will be free to develop more personal organizations.

The On-the-Job-Training Principle

Many people would like to do better with their lives. And they could if only they had someone to help them get started, or if they could see *you* doing business!

You can offer your downline associates on-the-job training by selecting the most interested of them to ride with you as you hold your seminars and meetings. As they work with you or as you hold meetings for them, they can see how you make your presentations. They can observe the closing phrases that you find effective. Have them tape record your conversations and copy the successful techniques that work for you.

As you know, enthusiasm is contagious! A big added benefit to this principle is that the associate working with you will be meeting other excited associates that you will be working with and will pick up on their successes.

Learning from your personal example and experience is far more effective than classroom-style training meetings.

The Short-Answer Principle

It is natural and good that people have questions, but they may sometimes ask questions that can draw them off the course of action they should be on. As a growing leader, learn to answer questions that are off the subject directly but briefly, and then lead the conversation back to where it should be—on results and result-oriented activity.

In many cases, when you answer in depth and with too much detail, the answer becomes unproductive because it was probably too much to absorb. Keep your answers to the point, and again, remember to lead the conversation back to reaching whatever objective you are working on.

The Leverage Principle

In networking, your job is not to move heavy objects, but to move people, and there are some very simple methods of natural leverage that can assist you in accomplishing this goal.

One example of leverage is for you to encourage your downline associates to attend motivational and training rallies with you. The speakers, the new ideas, and the electricity of the crowds are infectious. Many of your associates will be motivated by these events, and they will make stronger commitments to achieve their goals.

The Eat-an-Elephant Principle

How do you eat an elephant? One bit at a time! Remember this, and you will build a successful marketing organization for yourself in the same way—one associate at a time.

In a handy place, list the names and phone numbers of the associates that you sponsor. A good place to list them is on a convenient page in your appointment book. Put the names in pencil so that you can move the names of those associates who are the most active to the top of your list, and those who are less active toward the bottom of the list.

Why We Joined MLM
Jim and Connie Cardwell, Arizona

I was in real estate, earning more than $80,000 per year, when I first saw an MLM opportunity. Even though the idea of an ongoing income appeared to me, I wasn't excited about the product that was being sold. What got my attention to do multi-level marketing was a car accident that paralyzed me for one and a half years. During this time I had a lot of time to think. I realized that if I had gotten into multi-level marketing and worked it, I would still have had a continuing income.

The next time I saw an MLM opportunity, I was ready. Connie and I were living in a remote area, and a friend of ours was visiting us. As he walked in the door, he tripped, and a cassette tape fell out of his shirt pocket. When I asked him what it was, he said he didn't know. He said a friend of his had told him that it was about an opportunity to earn money. We listened to the cassette tape together that day, and we both liked what we heard. After checking the company out, we both got involved.

The toughest part of multi-level marketing is the fact that no one tells you to go to work because it is your own business. You have to be self-motivated. Therefore, we learned to have a minimum of one meeting per week. And, from our own experience, we learned to not prejudge anyone.

This is the same type of principle used by college or high school coaches when they list their first and second teams of athletes.

By using this system, you have a simple—but very effective—management tool that helps you to more objectively know with whom you should be spending your time. You will think more clearly and realistically about each person and the organizations that you are working with. It really helps to keep everything in perspective.

The You-Can't-Lose-What-You-Don't-Have Principle

This is a tough principle for most people to pick up on, but once you do, it will really work for you.

Here's the scenario: You have this great prospect at your seminar, and you are hoping he will join your business, but he is hesitating. At this point you should ask him to test market your business by inviting a few friends into his home. Unfortunately, many people are hesitant to ask prospects to do this for fear that they will lose them.

What it comes down to, is this—you can't lose them, because you don't have them in the first place! In other words, you have nothing to lose and everything to gain by asking your prospect to test the business. They will either react positively and begin to grow in your business, or they will decide not to become active. Either way, you gain, not lose, because if they decide *not* to become active, you know you are free to expend your energies elsewhere, and of course, ask them for referrals.

Another example might be that someone you sponsor is doing something or saying things that are upsetting to others. Don't be afraid to discuss this problem with him for fear of offending him thereby losing him. If you do not have a tactful, private conversation with him, you will eventually lose him anyway. You will probably also lose some other good people who decide that they don't need the hassle.

The Cup-of-Coffee Principle

A friend of yours offers you a cup of coffee, and you ask him for just one teaspoonful of sugar. Instead, your friend puts in three of four teaspoons. Obviously, your coffee is now too sweet, and the taste is diluted and changed.

As you hand out literature, cassette tapes, and other information in your networking business, don't give too much. If you do, you will dilute what you want your prospects or associates to see. More is not always better. It is better to give your prospect or associates two or three really good testimonial letters to read instead of ten. They are more likely to skim-read the ten and miss or dilute the value of the two or three good letters.

Why We Joined MLM
Tom and Barbara O'Toole, California

My introduction to multi-level marketing came as a result of my teaching marketing at National University in San Diego, from which I had graduated with an MBA in business education. One of my students mentioned an MLM opportunity to me, and initially I thought it was beneath me. After I checked into it, though, I realized the potential it had. How else can you start your own business with such a small investment?

I approached my entry into multi-level marketing as I would teach anyone in a marketing class, with these points in mind:

1. Set goals.
2. Do not plan to get rich quick.
3. Investigate the company you will be involved with.
4. Develop a plan of action, and stick to it.

If you are going to be involved, even on a part-time basis, approach it with the same dedication and motivation as if you were starting your own company. This is, in fact, exactly what you are doing!

The two most common mistakes I see in multi-level marketing are the following:

1. People dropping out before giving it a chance to work.
2. Stressing features of your product or opportunity instead of the benefits.

Just like other areas of Multi-Level Marketing, it is very important to stay focused on the fundamentals that are productive and to not dilute your efforts.

The Word-Picture Principle

"A picture is worth a thousand words." How many times have you heard that? But it *is* true, so talk in pictures, stories, and examples. Use word pictures, and more people will be able to relate to you; use stories and examples, and more people will better understand what you are trying to teach them.

The "Sibkis" Principle

"See It Big, Keep It Simple!" This is important to you! Work toward the bigger profit, and you will more likely get there by keeping your business-building techniques simple. In other words, use techniques that are simple enough to be duplicated by a large number of people.

Say the number 1,000 out loud. Now say 100 out loud. Was it any more difficult to say 1,000 versus 100? So why not add 1,000 new associates to your downline instead of 100! How? Find ten people in your downline who can see themselves bringing in 100 people each. And that totals 1,000 for you!

The First-Priority Principle

You are tired. You have just arrived home and see that you have four phone calls to return to associates. You also have two prospects that you need to call and set appointments to see.

Most people will make their four backup phone calls first. When you develop this habit, in many cases you will then put off making the phone calls to your two prospects until a later date, or never.

The principle here is that you develop the habit of making the phone calls to your prospects first, then make your four backup phone calls. By following this system, in 95 percent of the cases you will end up making all your phone calls, including the most important ones—those to your prospects. The only exceptions to this rule are emergency phone calls.

The Do-It-Now Principle

How do you handle procrastination? This is a problem everyone faces to one degree or another. Here are two simple solutions to help overcome procrastination.

1. The first comes from a suggestion made by the multimillionaire businessman W. Clement Stone. He states that if you repeat, "Do it now, do it now" five to ten minutes each morning and then again each afternoon, within two to three weeks you will overcome procrastination. As silly as this idea sounds, it actually works.

2. Make a do-it-now list each day. Number each item on your list in order of importance, and cross each item off as you accomplish it.

Why I Joined MLM
Richard de Vasto, Florida

After 24 years in the Marine Corps, I retired as a first sergeant. I then worked as a U.S. federal marshal and had a floor-covering business before becoming a realtor, mortgage broker, and investor.

With multi-level marketing I saw an opportunity to build a business with an unlimited income potential without high overhead. Overhead is a killer for the small businessman.

You can develop a recurring income with multi-level marketing. As long as you work for someone else, that person controls your time and income. In many cases that results in your working just hard enough not to get fired, while you're being paid just enough so that you don't quit! And *that's* a rut! The Bureau of Labor Statistics states that 81 percent of all working Americans are discouraged with their jobs, but they don't have enough confidence to make a change. With MLM, you have an opportunity to begin a new career, even part time. The only qualification that you need is a strong desire to succeed.

Your attitude and not your aptitude determines your altitude. With MLM you have a support group to help you. Procrastination is the thief of time and the graveyard of opportunity. Do it now, and remember, results do not determine attitudes—attitudes determine results!

The Taproot Principle

From an acorn, a great oak grows! Feeding a giant oak tree are literally hundreds of miles of roots under the ground. Among these roots is what is called the taproot.

The taproot goes deeper into the earth than the other roots. Its purpose is to tap a water supply deep in the earth that is not affected by dry seasons and droughts. A taproot will sustain the life of a tree during a dry spell.

In multi-level marketing, when you sponsor a new associate, one of your objectives is to develop a "taproot" in your new associate's downline.

Your objective is to find a person in your downline organization who will consistently produce new business. Let's say

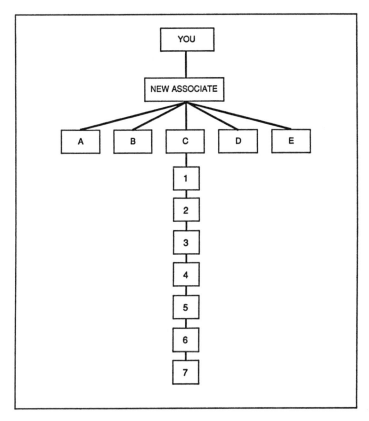

Taproot Principle

for example, in the following diagram, that number 7 is that key person. Each time number 7 places new business, it creates profits and motivation for each person in the upline, from C to 6, including the new associate and even yourself.

Number 7 effectively becomes your "taproot" in C's downline organization. If people in the upline from 7 have a "dry spell," 7's consistent new business will help to keep the others alive.

The Give-Before-You-Ask Principle

One of the key reasons people join a good MLM opportunity, besides income potential, is recognition and independence. They are looking to become independent, in other words, be their own boss.

There is certain information that as an upline you need to keep up with. There is a right way and a wrong way to ask for that information. The wrong way is to just call and ask for it, for example:

1. Joe, how much business volume will you have this week?
2. Joe, how many guests do you expect to bring to the next meeting?
3. Joe, have you followed up on Bill yet?
4. Joe, will you do the product part of the meeting tomorrow night?

The right thing to do when you call Joe, is to first give him some information or tips, then ask the preceding questions. For example:

1. Joe, did you hear that Harry just sponsored two new associates?
2. Joe, have you heard how to present the new product yet?
3. Joe, I want to let you know how proud I am of you and the way you put on the last meeting.
4. Joe, may I have your address, I have a dynamite testimonial letter to send you!

What I am suggesting here is that whenever possible, make an attempt to compliment and inform your downline (give) before you ask questions. You will find your future phone calls most welcome when you use this approach.

MLM Success Profile:
The Leslie and Grant Carney Story

"Grant and I had gone to high school together and were reacquainted at our ten-year class reunion. At that time, Grant was working as a geologist, but now he works full time with me in Herbalife," says Leslie.

"I started my MLM career while I was still single. I had moved to a new city and had decided not to continue working as a dental hygienist," she continues. "So I answered an ad and went to a meeting. I have to admit that I had a negative feeling at first, but because I needed to make some money to pay my bills, I decided to try the Herbalife MLM opportunity.

"I became motivated when I began meeting people who didn't have any special abilities who were earning a lot of money. This naturally caught my attention, and it motivated me to put forth extra effort. The extra effort paid off, and I earned over $2,000 during my first month. I thought, 'Hey, this is great! I'm making more money now than on a *real* job; my hours are my own; I'm my own boss; and I have the freedom that I want.'"

Leslie is quick to add, "Some people come to meetings and hear success stories. Many of them think they will make money without working at it. They get pumped up, buy a kit, but don't go to *see* anyone.

"I decided to move back to Canada, and while I was there I worked day and night," Leslie continues. "Was the effort worth it? For me it was! We have the income, the life style, and the freedom to live where we want to live.

"We have a six-figure annual income spanning several countries, and we live in Colorado! Our MLM business is truly an international one. We receive 60 to 70 percent of our income from Canada, England, Scotland, Ireland, and Australia.

"The last seven years have been a dream come true. I've flown on the Concorde to Paris and vacationed in the south of

France," she says. "There have been trips to Hawaii, Mexico, the United Kingdom, Australia, Hong Kong, Singapore, and Tahiti.

"When I started this business, many people said that I wouldn't do well. Instead of letting that discourage me, I set out to prove them wrong. I worked hard, and it has *definitely* paid off," Leslie concludes.

Leslie and Grant's Keys to Success

In general, stick with one company. Be consistent with your efforts. Work hard. Give others confidence. Communicate with key leaders and new people. Conduct organizational meetings. Respect company leadership. Run ads, hand out flyers, and talk to lots of people.

Some of the things that we have done are more specific:

1. Ask people where they are from. Some people have friends or relatives in foreign countries. We help follow up on their people and others throughout the United States.

2. We maintain a good retail business. We ship our products to retail customers all over the country. This adds to our profit and sets a good example for our downline; as a result of this, we sponsor new associates from satisfied customers.

3. We try to pinpoint a new associate's motivation factor, and then we work to keep him or her on that track.

4. There are two key phrases that are very important to us in our MLM business.

   a. Lawrence Thompson, our company's Executive Vice President for Sales, told us, "In the land of the blind, the one-eyed man is king." This phrase gave me confidence when I felt inadequate because of my young age or inexperience. Each new person should realize that he or she knows more than their brand-new prospect.

   b. When you hear negatives about your product or company, realize that it's 90 percent opinion. Don't let negative people slow you down!

Chapter
5

DELEGATE, DELEGATE, AND DELEGATE SOME MORE

Let's assume you want to build a large MLM organization—maybe 200, 500, or even 2,500 people. You know you're good, and you want to enjoy the big income, status, security, and power that come with creating a highly successful networking family.

But how are you going to do it? Even though you are cured of "time excusitis," there are still only 24 hours in a day. And even though you have a high energy level, you only have so much get up and go!

Here is the point: To build a large, successful MLM family—your ultimate goal—you must master the principles of delegation. You must learn to divide your "family" into small groups and duplicate yourself by putting a competent person in charge of each group.

Look at these advantages of delegation:

1. *Prompt assistance when new people need it.* MLM organizations are dynamic. As your family grows, new people join the group every week. New people need immediate help when they experience difficulty in selling the product, making appointments, or even processing the paperwork. So it is vital that competent assistance be quickly available. This much is certain regardless of how promising the newcomer appears; that person will not last long unless, through delegation, you supply someone to give him or her immediate skill, know-how, and moral support. Most people, if left alone to sink or swim, will sink.

2. *Delegation gives experience to your support people.* It is important to remember that the more effective your downline leaders become, the more volume they will generate and the more money you will earn. Your downline managers learn by doing. They may handle situations differently from you, and

they will make mistakes. But delegation of authority to act is the only way they will become experts as business builders. Nothing builds confidence in a downline manager faster than being told, "John, you can handle it," or "Jean, work it out the best way that you can."

3. *Better decisions often result when the downline leader makes them.* Your downline is usually closer to the people he or she recruits. He or she knows the recruit's family situation, work environment, habits, skills, and other characteristics that make the person unique. So he or she is often in a better situation to make the very best decision on a matter.

4. *Delegation frees you to think strategically.* To build a big organization requires a lot of big thinking. When you delegate properly, you have more time to think about make-or-break questions such as:

"How can I recruit more successfully?"

"How can I retain more of the people who sign up with me?"

"How can I better demonstrate the advantages of networking?"

"How can we sell more of our product?"

Your downline people have a right to expect you to innovate to solve major problems, to discover ways for them to earn more money, and to help them to build their businesses. To be great in networking or in any activity, you must spend some time alone so you can plan.

> He who every morning plans the transactions of the day and
> follows out that plan carrys a thread that will guide him
> through the labyrinth of the most busy life. But where no plan
> is laid, where the disposal of time is surrendered merely to the
> chance of incident, chaos will soon reign.
>
> *Victor Hugo*

How to Delegate in Multi-Level Marketing

Once you see the practical wisdom in delegating authority, the next consideration is *HOW?* Delegation is always an *art*, never a science. Each Networker has his or her own style. What works for another person may not work for you, and vice-versa.

Why We Joined MLM
Tod and Nancy Aldrich, Minnesota

I graduated from the University of Southern Minnesota with a triple major. I taught at the University, but later Nancy and I moved to Colorado, where I invested in a health and handball club, two hotels, a funeral home, an ice cream store, an antique store, and some real estate.

A lady who bought a house from my real estate company gave me a cassette tape to listen to. On this tape was an MLM opportunity. I can't believe now that I had missed out on MLM for so long. I had heard about MLM years before, but I didn't think it was a professional opportunity, because I never took the time to understand it.

What I see in MLM is that it gives you an opportunity to identify people who are producers, and this can reward you financially throughout your lifetime. MLM can give you a continuing income. When I sell a piece of property, for example, I make a profit, but only once.

Men and women are equal in MLM, and no special education or talent is needed. In what other field but multi-level marketing can nothing but persistence and enthusiasm pay you over and over again?

There are four important guidelines that will help you to become a good delegator:

1. *Have the courage to delegate.* Some MLM leaders are afraid to delegate. They feel that the person to whom they assign responsibility won't perform satisfactorily, and this will make them, personally, look foolish.

Delegation does involve risk. But risk is inherent in your job as an MLM leader. The key to minimizing this risk is to delegate to the right people.

Some networkers won't delegate because they fear the person to whom they delegate will outshine them. This attitude is foolish, of course, because the better job your downline people do, the more you will earn.

2. *Delegate to the right people.* No two people in all of creation are exactly alike. This makes it impossible to draw a profile of the perfect person to whom you can delegate. Nevertheless, as you delegate, consider the following qualities:

a. *Enthusiasm.* Enthusiasm is contagious! And since in the ideal MLM family you *want* everyone to be enthusiastic, you need to put people in charge who are enthusiastic, love the business, and see its potential.

b. *Experience.* People who hold or who have held responsible jobs have had experience in accepting and carrying out authority. Some of the most successful networkers have held positions of responsibility in the military, government, education and industry.

   On the other side of the coin, though, there are many people who were held back from responsible jobs in industry because of lack of education, age, race, sex, or wrong timing. Many of these people, when given the opportunity of multi-level marketing, excel at leading others. All they needed was the chance.

c. *Desire.* When one of your networking family tells you, "Let me handle them," or "Give me a chance to try," you know the person has desire. So consider people who volunteer. Let them show the marketing plan, relate their personal experiences to a group, or share ideas.

3. *Define the specific results you expect.* Never delegate in vague generalities. Look at these contrasts, and learn to be more specific.

Vague	*Specific*
Improve sales volume.	Increase sales by x units.
Add more people to your downline.	Add 15 new people to your downline within 30 days.
Do a better job of retaining your people.	Keep your downline family loss ratio below x percent.

4. *Stand by the person to whom you've delegated the authority.* Remember, you can delegate *authority*, but you can't totally delegate responsibility. Once you've delegated respon-

sibility, you must be ready to help that person if he or she needs it. In a way, your relationship with the person to whom you've delegated a task is like your relationship with a teenager.

A wise parent delegates ever-increasing responsibility to a teenager but is always there when a big problem arises. So it is in networking. You must always be willing to lend a hand when your support person gets in a tough situation. *You* must be *their* support person!

> *When you find a man who knows his job and is willing to take*
> *responsibility, keep out of his way and don't bother him with*
> *unnecessary supervision. What you may think is co-operation*
> *is nothing but interference.*
>
> *Thomas Dreier*

Your Persuasive Skill Is a Must

Most people work for an employer as an employee. But in multi-level marketing, you are not an employer, and your support people are not your employees.

This difference is significant. The law governing employer-employee relationships is based on an old Roman law that spelled out how a master could treat his slaves.

Although the master–servant law has been liberalized many times, today an employer still has power to order, require, compel, demand, and insist that his decisions be carried out by his employees. The employer decides who will be employed, what employees will be paid, what their working conditions will be, the work they will do, when they will work, the physical environment in which they will work, and who their associates will be. Employers also decide who will be promoted, demoted, transferred, and terminated.

Employers, then, have legal power to delegate. If an employee does not accept the delegation, he or she can be fired. In the networking relationship, there is no such power over people. Everything you accomplish as an MLM leader is achieved through persuasive appeal to a person's self-interest.

So as an MLM leader you must show your supporters that it is to their personal advantage to

1. Follow your guidelines for selling your product, recruiting people, and developing them into productive downline associates.
2. Use procedures you recommend for motivating their personnel.
3. Retain people who become discouraged.

Because you lack legal power to demand that your decisions be implemented, you must rely on your diplomacy, negotiation skill, and tact to move your organization forward.

Put Together a Small, Aggressive, Goal-Seeking Team

The challenge of building a great MLM empire is simpler than you may think. You need only a small number of people who share your dream and are willing to make the sacrifices needed to make it come true.

Andrew Carnegie built an enormous steel business. For many years he *was* the steel industry, and the most powerful industrialist alive. Once, in discussing his awesome success, Carnegie said something that is of enormous significance to people who want to build a networking empire: "You can take away my mills, my patents, my customers, and my money. But leave me my five key managers, and before you know it, I will again be number one."

The point Carnegie made applies directly to building an MLM organization. You can, with surprising speed, build a great multi-level business with only five people!

Look at the potential of only five dedicated individuals working with you. Five people can each soon build a team of ten. And each of these teams can build units of ten each. Now, in a reasonable period of time, you have in your group five leaders and 500 supporters.

But back up. Notice that all you did was recruit five able people, teach them the business, and get them excited. You probably spoke at many opportunity meetings and met many of the 500 who are now on your team. But the real work in creating your downline was done by your five key associates.

You, of course, have an ongoing responsibility to plan, organize, direct, and control the activities of your organization.

You want more people and more volume. A mark of leadership is continuous creative dissatisfaction. You will never stop asking two demanding questions:

1. "How can we do better?"
2. "How can we do more?"

As you consider multi-level marketing, you may be experiencing self-doubt. You may be asking, "Do I have what it takes? My record to date is rather ordinary. Somehow, I just can't see myself as head of a 500- or 1,000- or 2,500-member networking family."

You can go a long way toward curing self-doubt when you realize that the five team players have qualities you lack. Absolutely *no one* is endowed with all the ingredients of success. That's why you need to build a small team of enthusiastic people up front.

Why We Joined MLM
Jim and Carol Hendrix, California

Our daughter first told us about multi-level marketing. At the time I worked as a secretary, and Jim was working in the commercial construction field. Originally, I was not able to stand up and talk in front of others, so I relied on my enthusiasm. Both Jim and I have gained a lot of confidence and have seen a lot of personal growth in each other. We saw an opportunity to get into a new field and build a retirement income while keeping our present jobs.

We have developed an income that enables us to do some of the extra things in life. For example, we are able to do a lot more for our 17 grandchildren than we normally would be able to do. During the last four years in multi-level marketing we have developed a retirement income that is already approximately $150 more per month than Jim would receive from his union retirement plan after 30 years of working.

We have found that anyone can do this business if they are persistent.

Henry Ford was once involved in a libel suit with the *Chicago Tribune*. The *Tribune* had called Ford an ignoramus, and

Ford, a man of self-respect, said in effect, "Prove it." Lawyers for the *Tribune* asked him scores of simple questions such as, "Who was Benedict Arnold?" "When was the Revolutionary War fought?" and other questions, most of which Ford, who had little formal education, could not answer. Finally, Ford became quite exasperated and said, "I don't know the answers to those questions, but I could hire a man in five minutes who does."

Henry Ford was never interested in miscellaneous information. He knew what every major executive knows—*the ability to know how to get information* is more important than using the mind as a garage for unnecessary facts.

So regard your initial team of five as your brain trust. By working together you can solve any networking problem that may come up.

Great Networkers Are Like Generals—They Delegate!

For example, let's pretend for a moment that you are a general in the Army. You send a platoon of 100 soldiers out to the front lines of a battlefield.

But, there are no sergeants, lieutenants, or captains in this platoon. Just 100 soldiers. What will happen when the firing begins? Because there is no organization and no leadership, your 100 troops will prove totally ineffective. Some will hide. Others will desert. Still others will move in the wrong direction. And some will surrender. In the absence of leadership, a group of people, even highly talented ones, is simply a mob.

Many MLM leaders fail to organize their network of associates to move the business forward.

Now let's say you are an intelligent general. You are going to be a better leader and send your platoon of 100 soldiers to the front line with four good sergeants, two good lieutenants, and a great captain. This second platoon has leadership, and is more likely to hold its position, work together, and be successful for you.

The difference? Seven good leaders. Just as a general will delegate authority to junior officers to lead, train, and motivate his troops, the great network leaders also delegate authority to

their support people to help get the job done. In a phrase:
Delegate or stagnate!

When delegating, do not set up a chain of command, set
up a chain of counsel. More power rests with those in a position of *influence* than with those in a position of *authority*.

Successful networkers work closely with only a few carefully selected people—folks who are "fat":

> Faithful
> Available
> Trainable

Look for people with leadership qualities and desires and
spend extra time with them. As they mature and learn, they
will give direction to your downline associates.

Please understand this point. You may not become a general overnight, but you are more likely to reach the upper levels
of your MLM organization when you follow the principle of
working with a few good leaders.

Be Highly Visible

Learn a lesson from former President Ronald Reagan. Only a
few people in his administration had immediate access to him.
Yet the masses of people, even those who voted against him,
say they felt closer to him than to any other President in
history.

Why? Because Reagan made personal visibility a key part
of his Presidential style. Without fail, he talked to the American
people every week on the radio. And he spent much more time
in front of TV cameras than any of his predecessors.

To ensure visibility, at least one leading MLM leader has
his own private TV network so he can hold weekly meetings
with his "officers and personnel."

Just as a general will hold meetings occasionally with all
the troops under his command, you should hold meetings several times a year with all the people in your organization, especially your key leaders. Your downliners want to see you, listen
to you, and shake your hand. This builds their pride and gives
them an incentive to grow.

Start Growing—Now

Promote yourself. One way to grow is to take on responsibilities. Offer to help out at the meetings. Make yourself available to pick up and return guest speakers to the airport. By associating with leaders who are growing in the business, you can observe and copy their good habits.

A word of caution here: do not be gullible. Avoid "hero worship." Use your wisdom and good judgment to guide you in picking and choosing the most honest and moral leaders to emulate.

Expect Growth

A very simple principle of leadership is that as people in your organization see you growing, they are more likely to grow also. *Expect* your key people to follow through. Ask yourself, are you a lifter or a leaner? You will find that by taking pride in doing well with your business, a high percentage of your key people will also have pride in being associated with you and also in doing well.

Realize that no one, including yourself, can make another person successful. You can inspire, encourage, and teach, but ultimately the person you are working with will grow only if he or she desires to. Part of being a good leader is to *draw out* another person's desire to be independent, and this is another form of delegating, or if you wish, duplicating.

The bottom line is to stay away from those who are looking for handouts and spend time with those who desire to work out.

To Delegate, Communicate

Another form of delegating is communication. Your ability to communicate increases the involvement of others with you. It is most important to increase your ability to communicate your positive feelings and emotions. This is especially true when you are sharing business-building techniques, your ideas, and any kind of meeting information.

Hug People with Your Feelings

Your associates can feel your enthusiasm, or your lack of it. This is also true of your belief in your business, your sincerity, your empathy, and all other emotional qualities. Learn to "hug" people with your words and feelings.

Suggestions for Better Communication

1. *Talk with "word pictures"—in other words, stories.* Confucious said, "A picture is worth a thousand words." People will remember a story a long time after the facts are forgotten. Involve others in your stories with leading questions, good eye contact, and by staying to the point.

2. *Keep your presentation simple.* You've heard the expression, "You can't see the forest for the trees." MLM is like all other endeavors in the sense that, if you get into a lot of detailed explanations, you get a lot of detailed questions. But when you keep you presentation simple, a much higher percentage of people will understand what it is you are trying to communicate.

3. *Place a value on your life.* This is not an egotistical statement, but an important reality. Value the information you are sharing with others. You are *special*. You *deserve* to do well. Value and respect your rights, and a larger number of other people will as well.

4. *Place a value on each person in your organization.* They have a right to do well, also, and they are looking to you to assist them. Value this relationship! When you do, you will communicate and work with your associates with more of a commitment. How much money can an associate earn you? In some cases thousands or tens of thousands of dollars! Your next new associate is more likely to be the "big one" when you communicate your excitement and belief about your business to him or her.

5. *Third-person selling is as basic to multi-level marketing as to any other business.* Ask your satisfied customers for testimonial letters, and then show these letters to your prospects. *These testimonial letters communicate!* They sell! You do not have to wait for someone else to do this—you must take the lead.

6. *Ice breakers start the ball rolling, especially with your prospects.* As you meet with a prospect for the first time, begin personalizing and building your relationship quickly. For example, at some point early in your conversation, simply show a few pictures of your husband, wife, children, or grandchildren. Just two or three pictures. Don't overdo it. This will help your prospect to get to know you more personally.

7. *"United we stand, divided we fall."* This phrase couldn't be more true! As you meet with your prospects, try not to sit across from them, but beside them whenever possible. Use words and phrases like "we" and "let's," "You never know until you try," and "This is a *great* value," along with other words and phrases you will develop that move people to action.

8. *Mailing lists are imperative.* But many people make the mistake of putting as many of their downline associates as possible on their mailing list. If you do this, you unintentionally take away leadership from your key people.

Why I Joined MLM
Myron Smith, Georgia

I graduated from the University of Dayton with a master's degree in business. When I first became attracted to multi-level marketing, I had a position in industrial management.

Multi-level marketing gives a person a gradual way to enter the sales and marketing field. In my case, I began with a $59 starter kit. Now I do over $2 million a year in business.

The MLM system is actually very simple. We deal through *people* instead of through companies. MLM relates directly to volume. Would you rather make 10 percent of $1,000 wholesale or 50 percent of $100 retail?

A new person's objective should not be to go full time, but rather to take the edge off their finances. Most people could use an extra $5,000 per year. Since they are not going to receive this type of additional income from the company they work for, they can go out and create their own system with MLM to produce that additional income to help offset inflation.

It is important to find the right company for you, one that has a combination of retailing along with the wholesale business. As you look, remember that you can never substitute enthusiasm for sincerity. Stay away from the MLM "junkies." These are the people who keep jumping from company to company. They do several things at one time, but they end up with nothing.

This is very important: develop a mailing list of one or two key people in each of your lines of sponsorship, and ask each of these key people to communicate to their downline what you share with them.

Remember, to grow large in multi-level marketing, you should be helping others to develop their businesses. Build them up as leaders. Give them the spotlight. Encourage their downlines to look to them for support and communication.

What do you do when you have a person in a key position who does not communicate with his or her downline? The answer is very simple—find another key downline person to put on your mailing list. This would be someone who is dedicated and is trying to grow in the business.

This subject leads into a deeper discussion of management. Or, you may prefer the term leadership. Think and act. Spend time communicating with your leaders on the subject of communication.

Let them know that because it is impossible for you to communicate with everyone in their organization, you need their help. Through your discussions, they will begin to realize that they have a responsibility to pass on to their downlines what they receive from you. This is called *making things happen*. Wishing, hoping, fretting, and complaining all avoid the solution that normally can be found by discovering who your leaders are and working through them.

Some associates do things right, but they don't do the right things. One of your keys to delegating is finding people who learn to "do things right," but it is far more important to find people who will learn to "do the right things." For example, it is important to learn how to make a good presentation of your product and opportunity, which is "doing things right," but closing prospects to buy your product or join your business is far more vital to you—and *that* is "doing the right thing."

There are associates who come to meetings dressed well, and bring a prospect or two with them. But at the end of the meeting they do nothing but talk about how wonderful the company, the product, and the opportunity is. These associates may think they are "doing things right," but they actually need to learn to "do the right thing."

The *right* thing would be for him to lean his conversation to a point of conclusion. And the conclusion is *action*. The action here would be to set up a meeting to help his new prospect to begin his business.

Another example is the associate who is *too* helpful to his downline organization. This associate may feel he or she is doing things right by being very available to help the downline at any time, but the right thing to do is to *expect* the downline to be active in building its own businesses. The right thing to do then becomes to support their efforts.

Things Right	*Right Thing*
1. Invite prospects to weekly meeting.	1. Pick up prospects and take to weekly meeting.
2. Show opportunity and leave literature.	2. Show opportunity and fill out applications.
3. Invite a friend to meet with you by asking for a yes or no response.	3. Invite a friend to meet with you by asking for a choice of two dates.

The right thing to do is delegate, delegate, delegate—remembering to provide the necessary support. It is much better to be supportive than to be helpful!

MLM Success Profile:
The Cal and Irma Misemer Story

Cal Misemer grew up in a small southern Missouri town and married Irma shortly after graduating from high school. He was introduced to direct marketing when he told a cookware salesman that he "could not afford" a set of cookware. The cookware salesman proceeded to talk Cal into going to work part time selling cookware!

At 18, Cal Misemer started a love affair with marketing that is still exciting after 40 years. For 24 of those years, Cal ran his own cookware company, selling directly to the consumer.

He had set a goal to retire at 55 years of age, which he accomplished. After two years of retirement, however, Cal decided that, if he could find something exciting in the field of marketing that would allow him to build his own business at this own pace, he would try it.

A good friend from Oklahoma contacted Cal to share information about a new MLM company connected with Pre-Paid Legal Services, Inc. This company had decided to test market the use of multi-level marketing to sell its membership instead of its conventional direct-sales program.

Cal says, "It required three phone calls over a period of three weeks before I agreed to drive the 250 miles to Tulsa, Oklahoma to look at the MLM program my friend was so excited about. I, like so many others, had a negative opinion of multi-level marketing; therefore, I was very hesitant to make the trip. But I liked what I saw and heard at the meeting.

"These past four and a half years have been the most fun and rewarding of the 40 years I've spent in marketing," continues Cal. "Fun in that I've had the opportunity of learning about another area of marketing that has allowed me to play a part in the success of a growing number of others across the country. The number of memberships written through my organization now exceeds well over 50,000 and continues to grow. The financial rewards in the short four and a half years have produced a six-figure income for us that causes me to say, "Why didn't someone properly introduce me to the wonderful world of MLM 20 years ago?"

Cal and Irma have enjoyed trips to Hawaii, Las Vegas, an Arizona resort, and a cruise to the Bahamas. They also qualified for a vacation to Europe. All of the expenses for these trips were paid for by their company.

Cal and Irma's Keys to Success

When someone asks me to what I attribute the measure of success that I am enjoying, I tell them the following:

1. Realize that you are starting your own business and that its failure or success is entirely in your hands.

2. Understand that MLM is no different from any other business in the sense that building a solid, healthy business doesn't happen overnight. This means that constant exposure of your business over a period of time is required in order to find good people.

3. As cream always rises to the top, so will the serious-minded person in your downline organization. It is important to understand that the new person in MLM does not go to work for you. You are not his or her boss. They go to work for themselves, and if you are to realize a measure of success for introducing them into your MLM business, you must go to work for them, helping them to achieve their goals.

For years I have used the tried and proven 80/20 formula in building business leaders. This means that I spend 80 percent of my time with 20 percent of my achievers. I spend 20 percent of my time with the semi-active and inactive people. In time, your good people will show up, and you will learn how to recognize them.

In summary, I attribute the measure of my success to putting into practice one of the bottom-line fundamentals of MLM—when you find a person who will make the commitment in time and energy, then *work for that person*. Duplicate your time, energy, knowledge, and talent through others, and your fun and rewards are automatic.

Chapter
6

HOW TO HOLD MEETINGS

It's a beautiful, warm day, and you are strolling along a small freshwater lake. Have you ever wondered what keeps the water in that lake fresh? Why do other lakes become stagnant and smelly? Lakes that stay fresh do so because they are fed by freshwater streams, creeks, or perhaps a river. The fresh water is the lifeblood of the lake.

Just as fresh water is the lifeblood of that lake, recruiting new associates is the lifeblood of your MLM business organization. New people bring new excitement—and new excitement brings new growth. Most of this new growth will come from what MLM people commonly call "opportunity meetings."

What Is Your "Reason Why"?

What is your personal goal, objective, or "reason why" to hold opportunity meetings and to build your business? The stronger your "reason why," the stronger your recruiting efforts will be. Throughout this chapter we will share meeting objectives and techniques as well as thoughts on how to organize and build excitement. But the bottom line to whether or not your meetings will at some point become successful is that you have a strong *reason* to build them up.

Some associates prefer not to use the word "meeting." Instead they call their meetings seminars, get-togethers, rallies, training sessions, or conferences. Use whatever term best fits your business.

Types of Meetings

One-on-One

One-on-one meetings can happen wherever you are getting together with other people. From homes, restaurants, and ball games, to picnics, waiting rooms, and airplane flights—you name it. Most of your one-on-one meetings should be limited to 30 or 40 minutes. Depending on the situation, however, they may sometimes be longer or shorter.

Many of your one-on-one meetings are just a few minutes long. They are encounters in which you will ask a few leading questions and then leave your prospect with either a cassette or videotape. These tapes are normally in the hands of the prospect for 24 to 48 hours.

Small Groups

Most small-group opportunity meetings are held with usually two to six people in homes, restaurants, and offices. The small-group meeting is effective, and you will have a higher percentage of new people joining your business as a result of these types of meetings versus big-group meetings. This is especially true when you have a mix of one or two excited associates along with three or more prospects. The belief and excitement of your associates is contagious and will help to inspire your guests to join you. This type of meeting should usually be limited to 45 minutes—and *never* longer than an hour.

Big Groups

Big-group opportunity meetings are more generally held in hotels and other large meeting hall locations and involve 25 or more people. Timewise, these meetings should be somewhat shorter than the small-group meetings. Because of the larger crowd, the challenge to keep your guests' attention becomes bigger. One of the purposes of big-group meetings is to inspire more one-on-one and small-group meetings. The reverse is also true. The one-on-one and small group meetings should promote and lead to big-group meetings.

Another objective of the big-group meetings is to allow you, as a leader, to meet new downline associates and prospects. The larger your organization grows, the more important it is for you to circulate at these functions to find new people to work with.

Rallies

In addition to the opportunity meetings, most companies or upline leaders hold motivational and training rallies on either a monthly or quarterly basis. The number of people attending rallies can range from around 100 to, in some cases, as many as 20,000 people. These functions are extremely important to the success of your organization, because in most cases, they will inspire your downline to *think bigger.* Many associates leave a rally with a stronger conviction about the business. As you listen to the success stories, you and your downline will tend to identify with at least some of the speakers. This will usually motivate your associates to build a business much bigger than they might normally have built.

The cost of attending a rally is normally the price of a movie and is well worth it, especially when you realize that the rally is designed to assist you in motivating your people.

Conventions

Most MLM companies will hold an annual national or regional convention. These serve the same purpose as that of a rally—motivation and training—but on an expanded basis. It is important, however, that you watch your expenses. Don't become a person who lives to attend one rally or convention after another. You should not be attending to catch some sort of magic idea. Your reason for attending should be to obtain new ideas and motivation. *That* is the purpose.

Franchise restaurant owners invest literally thousands of dollars in their businesses. You will make an investment in your MLM business also—an investment called *time.* We all have more time on our hands than we realize, and it is important to leverage time to make it work as efficiently as possible for you.

Why We Joined MLM
Greg and Dolores Jensen, Utah

I was the president of a wholesale food company and the owner of some tax-return franchises.

My first reaction to MLM was positive for the concept, but negative for the company I saw. Later, my first experience with MLM was bad because the company I joined went under. Because of this bad experience, I swore off MLM forever. I could never forget the concept though. I liked the idea that you could produce and make more by multiplying yourself through others. Later I came across a solid company, and I have been very happy with the results.

With MLM you are an independent agent. You can build a business the way that *you* want to build it as long as you stay within the company's concept. No one can pass you up in your organization. You can live where *you* want to live and still run your business. There are greater legal tax savings in MLM than in almost any other business that I know of. The satisfaction of helping people is very high in MLM.

Your Time Bank

What if you had a bank that credited your account each morning with $86,400? But no balance was carried over from day to day, and no cash could be retained in your account. Furthermore, every evening the bank canceled whatever part of the amount you had failed to use during the day. What would you do? Why, you'd draw out every cent, of course!

Well, you *do* have such a "bank." And its name is "time." Every morning it credits you with 86,400 seconds. Each night it rules off, as lost, whatever seconds you have failed to invest to good purpose. This account carries over no balances and allows no overdrafts. If you fail to use the day's deposits, the loss is yours, as there is no drawing against tomorrow. Put a *value* on your time, just as you do your money, and apply your time wisely as you hold meetings in your business.

Guidelines for Holding Opportunity Meetings

Introductory Remarks

Tell your audience that you are going to answer three basic questions at your meeting:

1. Is the company any good?
2. Is the service or product you are offering good?
3. Can you make any money at it or fullfill your dreams?

Do's and Don'ts

The content of your meeting is important, but it is equally important that your meeting be structured to flow naturally from your opening to your closing remarks. The following guidelines will be helpful to you:

1. Start on time. 7:30 or 8:00 p.m. for evening meetings is usually a good time.
2. Set up extra chairs *only as you need them*. A roomful of empty chairs is a negative sign, but it adds *excitement* when you need to set up more.
3. Turn the TV and stereo off.
4. Serve store-bought cookies or cake with coffee and/or tea. Fancy spreads intimidate people. There may be someone there who would like to join your business and hold a meeting, but they don't feel they have the time or money to do the refreshments. Keep it simple!
5. Keep it informal. It is important to let your guests serve themselves. And remember, no one is offended if you do not have alcoholic beverages, but someone might be offended if you do.
6. Post a "No Smoking Please" sign at the front of the meeting room. It will be respected and is generally appreciated, especially if the room is small.
7. Keep young children and pets out of sight during the meeting.
8. Dress neatly.
9. Allow people to browse through a brochure or product display either before the meeting or after your presentation—use your best judgment.

Objectives

You should work to accomplish four basic objectives at your opportunity meetings. Remember, though, not to get too fancy. Keep it simple and exciting, and keep your meeting moving toward your major objective, which is to sign up your prospects.

1. *Warm-up.* Circulate; shake hands and meet the people before the meeting begins. This relaxes your guests, encour-

ages your associates, and gives you an opportunity to get a feel for the crowd. It also gives you time to get to know your newer associates and guests and to see to whom you would like to spend time giving training tips after the meeting is over. This is important—you are looking for potentially dedicated people; invite them to have coffee with you after the meeting.

One more key point: many guests are uneasy when meeting new people. To help them to relax, make the following statement to each guest: "We're glad to have you here this evening. You are going to find this opportunity very interesting. If you have any questions, come see me after the meeting, and I will be glad to answer them for you."

2. *Presentation.* Create natural attention and interest with your opening comments. Proceed to explain your opportunity simply—*not* with an atmosphere of *education*, but with the expectation that people will be interested. Be sincere, not pushy. Keep on track. Stay off of tangents. Search for a leader in your company who is successful, and copy his or her pattern. It is extremely important to realize that most guests will not totally understand your opportunity the first night, so don't try to explain every little detail. Some people try to "explain the explanation"; instead, just hit the highlights, and help your guests to see the big picture.

3. *Close.* Your close should be aimed at getting prospects to join your business. Whether you are closing by signing guests at the end of your meeting or by giving them materials to take home so that you can follow up within the next day or so, the important point is to involve your guests in your business. This should be a process of leading people, not pushing. A simple method is to help people fill out their applications. Reword the following closing statements to fit your personality: "How many of you like to save time? (Raise your hand, and they will raise theirs.) We all do, and we're going to do something *now* to save time. We're going to take two to three minutes to fill out these applications so that they are completed properly. There is no obligation in filling these out, because they can't be processed until you sign them. By completing these now, you will save time in trying to get together later with the person who invited you. If you want to think about

this for a day or two, that's fine. You can take the completed application with you, and write a check to join later. Or, if you prefer to write a check tonight, that's fine also. First of all, fill in your name here. . . ."

If you are in a product-oriented business, for example, you may wish to hand your prospects a sample product order form to take with them, along with a checklist of items they would like to sample.

You may need to create a different type of close for your MLM business, and as you do, remember the key is twofold.

  a. Keep it simple, so that it can be duplicated.
  b. Find a close that consistently brings good results. A good close will increase the percentage of new people who join your organization.

4. *Follow-through.* Observe the people you meet at your meetings. Choose one or more people to spend additional time with after the meeting. These will be people who ask you questions or in some manner express a deeper interest in the business. Often, the *real* meeting starts *after* the meeting!

This is a great time to set up in-home meetings with new associates. This is a time when they are asking questions and are receptive to learning more about how to build their businesses. You can help them to review goals and assist them in setting up their meeting schedules. Keep yourself focused on the purpose you are there to fulfill. You are at the meeting to be productive and to help others become productive.

Why We Joined MLM
Ron and Nancy Dietrick, New York

My wife and I both teach special education. Nancy teaches elementary school, and I teach in a middle school. We found that we can do both our regular job and MLM simultaneously. The extra income from MLM gives you the things you *want*, because you are already supplying the things that you *need* with your regular income.

I was not interested when I first saw MLM because I saw it as selling. But Nancy *was* interested. My interest was sparked when we sold several hundred dollars worth of product during our first week. Then we sponsored six people into the business and waited six months for them to do something. During this period, I got serious and began holding meetings. Originally I saw MLM as a way to supplement our teaching incomes. Later we realized that we could create a total third income!

I like the freedom, the hope, and most of all the challenge of helping others that MLM offers. In MLM, I can still be a teacher, working with motivated adults who want to better themselves. Unfortunately, it is also very easy to let it slide, so I stress that it is extremely important to treat it as a business, and work on a schedule.

Attending rallies and other opportunity and training functions can be very beneficial. Here are some tips that will assist you in getting the most from any meeting:

1. *Sit as close to the front as possible so that you retain a high percentage of what is being presented.* Encourage your downline to do the same. And go early, it's well worth it. Meet and associate with the leaders; talk to them. Ask them questions, and *listen* to their answers. Write down notes. Find out *why* they are leaders.

2. *Promote!* The more people who attend the rally, the bigger your own business will grow. Remember that it's a numbers game. The higher the number of people at your meeting, the more potential prospects you have.

3. *Introduce yourself.* Meet others who are growing in the business. Don't be afraid to ask questions. The only dumb question is the one that wasn't asked. As you get to know people better, you will begin to identify with them and realize that most of them do not have any abilities that you yourself don't have. You will observe that they were just consistent in using their time and funneling their energies into building their businesses. You will begin to understand that if they can do it, you can too.

4. *Record the meeting.* Later, play the tape back at least two or three times, and you will pick up many good ideas that you may have missed the first time around.

5. *Ask the key leaders where the meeting after the meeting will be.*

6. *Seek out key leaders before the meeting, during the breaks, and after the meeting.* Ask questions; listen and take notes.

Tips for Making Your Opportunity Meetings More Productive

Most of your opportunity meetings will be one-on-one or small-group meetings. The following tips will help to make your meetings much more successful.

1. It is a fact that 100 percent of the people you pick up in your car and bring to a meeting will show up. But for the ones who do *not* show up at the meeting, follow up the next day by dropping off a cassette or videotape for your no-show guest to listen to or view.

2. When inviting a guest, ask for a commitment to attend your meeting. A typical response to your invitation might be, "I'll try to make it." This is a polite way of putting you off and is simply handled by your replying, "If you can't come, that's okay, but I would like to know for sure since I'm just inviting a few people. Would you mind checking your calendar (or with your husband/wife) while we're on the phone?" This will usually give you a definite commitment. And remember, if they discover they cannot come, set an appointment to drop off a cassette or videotape, at their house, while you are still on the phone.

3. Leave your guests with a cassette or videotape to study after they've gone home. This is important, because what you leave them will reinforce what they have heard at the meeting. Understand that sometimes your guests will go home feeling good about what they've heard. Unfortunately, they may receive negative input from someone else, or they might just get cold feet. Lending them some tapes will reinforce the positive aspects of what they heard.

4. When inviting a guest, ask each one to bring someone with them. This deepens their commitment and can

help them to get off to a much quicker start. Try saying, "Mary, why not invite a friend to come with you to-morrow evening. You can get his or her opinion and of course if your friend becomes interested, you will also benefit."

5. It's not the *manner*, but the *matter* in how you make your presentation that makes the difference. The same principle goes for inviting people to your meeting. The tone of your voice, your conviction, and your excitement will convey to people that you *expect* them to come to your meeting. And with this attitude, a higher percentage will!

Recruiting Tips

Rule 1: Do Not Prejudge Anyone

People you would never expect to be interested in MLM will surprise you with their excitement and their interest.

It is important to write down the names and phone numbers of anyone and everyone that you can think of. Again, do not prejudge. Just list each name as it comes to your mind.

Rule 2: "You Never Know Until You Ask"

Some people have more trouble making phone calls than others do. There are various points and approaches shared in this book that will help you to relax when you make your calls.

Do not try to get people interested over the phone. The purpose of the call is only to set an appointment.

Keep your wording simple and natural. Make it fit your personality. Encourage yourself to read your approach *out loud* several times so that it becomes more comfortable to you.

In most cases the person you've called will set the time for you to come by. Occasionally you will be asked, "What's it all about?" "It's about making money. The information on the tape may not be of interest to you, but it's worth a look. May I drop it off tomorrow evening, or is this evening better?" (You may wish to name the company or organization you are with.)

The key wording here is "it may not be of interest, but it's worth a look." And the choice of two times to stop by lends immediacy and importance to the opportunity.

You may sometimes use an approach asking for their opinion, "Carl, I've just seen a business opportunity and would like to get your opinion." Then give a choice of two times to drop off a cassette or videotape.

Why We Joined MLM
Vernon and Belinda (Spizzy) Pike, Georgia

I served for ten years in the Navy as an aviation electrician first class. During many of these years, my wife worked as a bookkeeper.

Initially we were both turned off by MLM because we didn't see anyone making money. We later met someone who was business-oriented in his approach to MLM, and therefore very profitable. He did not have a fly-by-night attitude to making money, and he showed us how he steadily grew more profitable each year in MLM with a proven game plan.

It was originally my business. Spizzy became interested eight months later when she saw that I was not going to quit, that the money was good, and that other people were genuinely interested in our success.

We studied and found out how our successful friend went about doing his business. We plugged into his system and ideas. We copied him and became very profitable, along with earning wonderful vacations and bonus cars.

Rule 3: The Three-Foot Rule

Anyone who is within three feet of you becomes a prospect. Realize that you are in the marketing business. Whether you realize it or not, you are constantly coming into contact with people who are prospects for your MLM business.

You will meet your prospects at work, after work, at restaurants, in elevators, at ball games, at church, at social functions, in stores . . . the list of places is endless. Some of the people you approach will be interested, and some won't. If you're wondering how you will know whom to ask, the answer is *everyone*.

Here is a simple approach that is not offensive to anyone:

YOU   Excuse me, may I ask you a question?

PROSPECT   Yes.

YOU   You like to save money, *don't you?* (Remember to emphasize *don't you* to draw a yes response while nodding your head and smiling.)

The key here is to not keep bugging a person to see your business opportunity when it is evident that he or she is not interested in listening.

It is taught in the Dale Carnegie Sales Course that there are five steps to making a sale:

1. Attention
2. Interest
3. Conviction
4. Desire
5. Close

It is important to gain someone's attention and interest first, before explaining the details of your business.

Some of your friends will be interested whether you talk to them or not. The point is that someone in MLM will contact your friends sooner or later, and if your friends are going to be interested, it might as well benefit *you.*

The following meeting-building concept is one of the most important things that you can learn from this book. Copy this concept in building your downline organization and eventually it will become a habit.

First, though, let's discuss what most associates in MLM normally *do* and then we will discuss what they *should* do. This is very simple to learn. Most associates normally try to:

1. Attempt to sponsor a lot of people personally, but not help them to be sponsors themselves.
2. Sponsor a few new associates, hold a meeting or two to assist them, and then run on to sponsor more associates.

Let's now look for a moment at the following diagram. You have personally sponsored associates A through E. What is done many times with new associates is to sponsor someone

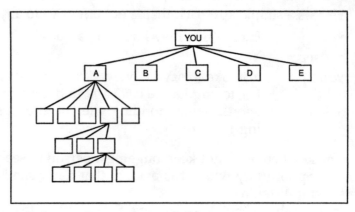

new, tell them what to do, and then run on to the next associate. This leaves you with excited but frustrated people.

What we should learn to do is as follows:

1. Hold at least one meeting for each new person. As you
    do this, you will discover that some of the new people
    will respond favorably and others will respond with
    less interest than you would like.

2. Let's say, for example, that A invites a number of
    guests to her meeting, but B and C do not. The spon-
    sor's natural instinct would be to think A is excited, I
    won't have to work with her. They will normally spend
    their time helping B and C to get started.

What you should do is just the opposite, work with A and her
downline, and instead of just forgetting B and C, invite them
and their few associates to come to meetings with you in A's
downline. By continuing to hold meetings downline from A,
you build a taproot. By building depth in A's downline, it will
normally motivate the upline to do more business. By bringing
B and C and a few of their associates with you to A's meetings,
you are helping them (instead of forgetting them), but at the
same time, you are concentrating on making A solid and profitable in your business.

Also, B and C hopefully will pick up the excitement of A's
meetings and wish to duplicate what they see and feel into
their own organizations. There is a saying, "monkey see, monkey do." Invite B and C to bring prospects with them to A's
meetings. As you understand what you have just read, you

will see that you can work with any number of personally sponsored associates at the same time.

As A becomes more confident and does more of the meetings in her organization by herself, you will find another key person to concentrate on, and of course, invite other semi-active associates to bring their guests to your next key person's meetings.

Remember, the tendency is to sponsor as many people as possible and tell them what to do. The more profitable technique is to sponsor a number of new associates, and concentrate your efforts by holding meetings for only the most active associates you have, and inviting the semi-active to come with you to the active meetings.

Many of your semiactive people will want what they see at the active meetings. They will also learn what you are doing and hopefully work to duplicate this excitement and business growth in their own downline organizations.

MLM Success Profile: The Shirley Green Story

Shirley Green is one of the many women doing extremely well in multi-level marketing. Over the years, Shirley was a licensed real estate agent and appraiser. She has also done geological drafting, mining exploration drafting, aircraft design drafting, and commercial art.

"When my husband, Fred [now deceased], and I first heard about Amsoil, hardly anyone had ever heard of synthetic lubricants. We were so excited about the product performance and potential that we could hardly talk of anything else.

"One of the things I enjoy most about my success and life style in MLM is all of the great friends I have made over the years throughout the world. It's wonderful to have a high six-figure income long with the opportunity to travel.

"I love the freedom to travel with this business, because, along with the opportunity to hold meetings and make a business profit, it seems that each person enjoys showing me what is unique to his or her area. This has resulted in some very interesting tours. For example, I saw two Broadway plays in New York City, and visited the Cartier jewelry store, Rumplemeyers ice cream parlor, and a little restaurant where aspiring opera singers are waiters and waitresses!

"I've also had tours of England, Scotland, Ireland, and Canada with Amsoil dealers who know those areas. On a business trip to Arizona, people who knew the area took me on a trip through the back roads explaining all about desert plants.

"I've not only been able to provide a comfortable living for myself, but I have been able to help a number of others as well. I helped my parents build an MLM business with Amsoil, and now that they are in their golden years at ages 80 and 73, they are quite comfortable. And they do *not* have to depend on social security, which is neither social nor secure!

"I have been able to help each of my four children to buy homes of their own. Recently I have been working with a program to provide houses for low- or no-income homeless people. The nature of MLM can provide not only the income for projects such as these, but also the freedom to take some time for these special projects," concludes Shirley.

Shirley's Key to Success

Being successful doesn't just happen. In multi-level marketing you learn to surround yourself with other success-oriented people. You do not have to necessarily sponsor people who travel in the fast lane, although it is nice to sponsor those who want to travel in the through-traffic lane. It is a *must* to find those who want to find the on ramp.

Persistence comes with commitment, and planning comes when you let your MLM business get into you. The biggest key is the decision to be successful and to not let anything or anyone steal that decision.

Chapter
7

SERVE YOUR CUSTOMER

"Try it, you'll like it" has been a popular phrase for years. It is extremely important that you try the service and/or products that your company offers. Become familiar with them, compare them with other competitive products/services, and find the things that you like about your products/services as you use them. Attend meetings that your company holds, and talk with other associates. By talking with others you will learn what they like about your product, and you will want to share what you learn and experience with friends, neighbors, and everyone who becomes your customer.

Many of your initial retail customers will be people you have invited to opportunity meetings. These people will come to look at an opportunity, and, in the majority of cases, they will buy your product or service.

Other customers will be the friends and neighbors who visit your home. Make it a point to use your product or service while they are visiting. As they observe you using it, more than likely they will ask about it, and this of course gives you a golden opportunity to show them what you have to offer.

Learn to make casual comments on how well the product or service works for you. Let your conversation be natural. You should not be "selling" your product, but you should be creating interest through these casual comments.

Show-and-tell is also a great approach. Lend a few products to friends to test market. When you do this, be sure to follow up within 24 to 48 hours. If you represent a service, create ways to demonstrate it to prospects and potential customers. This may take some ingenuity on your part, but it will be well worth the trouble.

One successful networker began his business by stopping by his neighbors' homes, offering to "give away" a name-brand product. He would ask each neighbor if he or she would like to have the rest of the product because his wife wouldn't use it anymore, having found something better. Naturally the neighbors would ask what she was now using, and of course he showed them!

Testimonial letters from satisfied customers are great door openers. Many of your customers will write you a letter, if only you will ask them to.

One of the keys to developing a good retail business is to not try to find a great number of customers yourself. Develop a few good and satisfied customers, and then ask for referrals. Call it word-of-mouth advertising or third-person referrals, but either way, asking for referrals works. Ask your customers to help you, and in most cases they will.

Most of these referrals will come one at a time, but you will find that they will add up. Some of your customers will allow you to do a home demonstration, which will help you to pick up several new customers at one time.

The most successful networkers are not afraid to ask others to help them out. The majority of your best customers will be those who come from referrals. With good service, these referred customers will stay with you for years. It is imperative to remember that it is far more important to ask for referrals than to try to develop some fancy system of trying to find all of your customers by yourself.

It is also important that you understand that no one benefits by only *knowing* about your product or service—they only benefit by *owning* it. *Ask* for the order! *You* have used your product. *You* have used your service. You believe in it. You know it works well. So it's important to realize that your customers can only benefit and enjoy your service or product by using it themselves.

It is amazing how many times you will find yourself talking with people about how terrific your product is, inwardly hoping that they will ask you to sell it to them. This is human nature.

Salesmanship consists of transferring a conviction by a seller to a buyer.

Paul G. Hoffman

Asking for the order can become a habit, just like *not* asking for the order is a habit that needs to be broken. One is a good habit and the second a bad habit. You work to develop better habits in other areas of your life, so why not work to develop the habit of asking for the order? You will be rewarded by developing the habit of closing sales.

> ### Why We Joined MLM
> *Vernon and Anne Glenn, Ohio*
>
> A lot of people miss what MLM can do for them because they go to a meeting and end up thinking that they have to make a lot of money to be successful. Vernon and I measure our success by reaching what *we* want, not by what someone else is achieving.
>
> Vernon has a good career as an industrial heating and air-conditioning technician. Upon entering MLM, I was working in direct sales. In MLM I have the freedom to find my own niche, to expand my horizons. You don't always have this opportunity with a job.
>
> I enjoy giving someone the same opportunity that I have. With MLM I can do that. As *they* grow, it helps *your* success. With some companies, you may help a fellow employee learn everything that you know, and you may end up not having a job one day!
>
> In MLM, it's important to find a leader in your business that you can work with. One who doesn't push you to meet his or her goals, but who will help you to meet *your* goals.
>
> It is important that you not take the no's personally. Prospects are usually right. By leaving people with a good feeling, they are more likely to call you back when the timing is right for them to get involved with you and your opportunity.

One of your reasons for finding good customers is to be profitable, but part of being profitable is keeping your expenses down.

Once there was an "all-star," full of enthusiasm and energy, who ran all over town visiting customers and delivering products. See the following diagram.

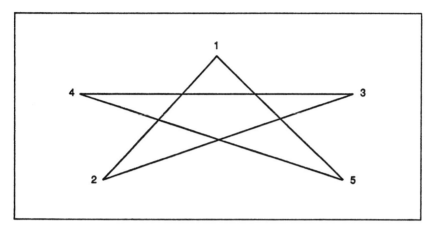

He energetically traveled from point 1 to point 2, proceeding on to points 3, 4, and 5. He became a featured speaker at meetings and rallies because of all the sales he was making.

In reality, however, the all-star became an all-star failure because he incurred heavy expenses and wasted valuable time by driving all over town.

The key here is to ask your customers at point 1 for referrals in their neighborhood and develop three to five more customers with that stop.

Build A Referral Lead System

A major problem many people have in MLM marketing is that they are dead in the water for new prospects when they run out of their "natural market" of friends, relatives, and people they know.

There is a simple solution to this problem, and it is called the "referral lead system." Each time you make a sale, you ask your client to write down ten referrals for you, and you ask each new associate to write down 25 names for himself. This takes a little extra time, but it will give you an endless source of leads.

The key here is for you to develop the habit of using this technique, and expect your downline associates to use it as well. You will create not only an explosion of new business, but also continual expansion of your business. The chart on page 105 is an example of a form that could be used by your new associate or customer to list referrals.

It is also very important to organize a follow-up system with your customers. A system is important so that you will have the time to sponsor and build yourself a profitable downline organization.

Keep your follow-up system simple. A 3 x 5 note-card file can be very effective. The basic information is all that is necessary. Do not bog yourself down with unnecessary details.

To help yourself be consistent with your follow-up service calls, mark special times on your calendar to make these back-up calls. Marking your calendar is a technique similar to making a list of things to do today, and it works!

Most of your more successful networkers will develop a simple system to follow up with their customers on a regular schedule and will spend the majority of their time sponsoring and building their downline organization.

In fact, many of their customers will come from people they show their business opportunity to. This concept is sometimes called "recruit to sell." This recruit-to-sell approach begins with a very simple question. For example, "You like to save money, don't you?" They ask this question or a similar one of everyone they come in contact with.

Many people will respond positively. You will share your opportunity with these people, hoping to recruit them into your business, but you will also make customers out of them at the same time. They may become one of your associates and a wholesale customer, or they will become a retail customer. Either way, you will have increased your business volume.

You may have some paperwork involved with your product or service. Learn to streamline this detail. For example, instead of handwriting thank-you notes, develop a form letter that looks sharp.

You will also find it to your advantage to follow a "do it now" philosophy. If you let details pile up, so will the pressure, and you will tend to become less productive. It is most important not to sit at home doing detail work when you should be out seeing prospects, customers, and downline as-

REFERRALS

New Associates / Client: _____

Sponsor & Phone Number: _____

	Referral's Name	Spouse's Name	Address	Ages	Telephone # Home / Work	Occupation	Key Reasons for Recommending
1							
2							
3							
4							
5							
6							
7							
8							
9							
10							
11							
12							
13							
14							
15							
16							
17							
18							
19							
20							
21							
22							
23							
24							
25							

sociates. Fit the detail work into a less busy time in your schedule.

Some people are great motivators, but poor on details. Instead of letting this become a negative attribute, delegate the details. This will free you to do what you do best.

Many associates pay their children to assist them. This is one way in which your business can become a family affair. And while your children are earning their own money and growing in responsibility, you are free to build your downline organizations.

Delegating the details is a big step toward providing excellent service to your customers. Probably the best promotion you can ever offer is good, dependable service. This can guarantee that you will build up and maintain a profitable customer base. A higher percentage of your customers will refer you to their friends when they know that they can depend on you.

The discipline of servicing your retail customers regularly serves several purposes:

1. Increased profits for you
2. Potential profits for you
3. A good example for your downline to follow
4. Experiences that will improve your ability to train others

---

Why We Joined MLM
Bob and Barbara Jackson, Florida

I got into multi-level marketing to earn an extra $100 a month. I worked for the State of Florida as a vocational education consultant for the Department of Education. I have done a lot of community service, and I look at MLM as doing a community service because I help people to help themselves.

It takes work, time, and effort. Since being forced into an early retirement by the state, I have developed an income double what my salary used to be. Plus my wife can assist me and we have the freedom of owning our own business. For 30 years of working in jobs, my time and income were controlled. Now I am able to do more for my

> family than ever before, like taking them to Hawaii, for example. It's nice to be able to take great vacations!
>
> For a while I made the mistake of helping people who didn't want to help themselves. The biggest danger I see in multi-level marketing is the MLM "junkie," who floats from business to business instead of finding one good company and sticking with it. My friends know that I'm serious and committed to my business, and therefore they keep referring other people to me.

It is important to maintain a balance between retailing and sponsoring. This is like rowing a boat. Let's say that the left oar is retailing and the right oar is sponsoring. If you pull on either one exclusively, you will go in circles.

Although it is important to concentrate on sponsoring to build a large organization, maintaining a good base of retail sales is also very important to your business. This is especially important when you realize that your downline organization will, for the most part, follow the example that you set.

The "Farm System" of Prospecting

A good farmer plants his seeds in the best land on his farm, and, with the proper follow-through, will normally reap a profitable crop.

Multi-level marketing is similar. You reap what you sow. If you "sow" or prospect only one person per week, you can only "harvest" one new associate or customer that week. On the other hand, if you prospect ten people, you stand a chance to sponsor up to ten new associates or sell to up to ten new customers that week.

One of your objectives then is to create more exposure in order to expand your ability to prospect larger numbers. One of the best systems to achieve this objective is the "farm system."

It's a very simple system. Begin by printing business cards and/or door hangers with the following message:

> *If you are tired of paying retail and would like*
> *an advantage, call 555-5555 for a two-minute*
> *recorded message.*

You may want to reword this example to more fit the personality of your business.

The farm system allows you to expose your business to a much larger number of prospects than normal. You meet people constantly through your everyday routine. You talk with people at the retail store, when you get your car repaired, at ball games, at offices you visit—there are as many different situations to talk to people as you yourself can create. Simply ask these people the leading questions that fit your business— "You like to save money, don't you?" or "You like bargains, don't you?"

As you ask your questions, smile, be relaxed, and slowly nod your head. Most people will say yes. Then you merely hand them one of your cards and state that you represent a company that provides a special kind of service or product, and ask them to call the phone number on the card for a two-minute recorded message that will explain the details.

Hand out the cards to everyone you meet. Put the door hangers out in nicer neighborhoods. The door hanger technique is one that is used very successfully by many different kinds of businesses. A word of caution here: do not place the cards on windshields of cars or in mailboxes, as this is illegal in many communities.

Plan to distribute hundreds of these cards or door hangers. The more exposure, the more phone calls you will receive. At this point your objective is to create a curiosity to hear the two-minute recorded message. You want potential prospects and customers to call. And you are trying to "sell" them or "close" them to make that phone call! A large number will call and listen to your message, because people do not feel threatened by listening to a recording. The phone number should be connected to an answering machine on which you will have the two-minute recorded message.

Remember that your initial conversation with the people that you give the cards to will normally be as brief as a minute or two. You can hand these cards to your dentist, your doctor, their receptionists, your hairdresser or barber, your dry cleaner, waiters and waitresses at your favorite restaurants— again, the list goes on and on.

Ask people to pass the card on to someone else after they have called the recorded message. You may be able to think of many creative ways to multiply your efforts with the farm system.

Why We Joined MLM
Roger and Becki Laverty, Georgia

I joined multi-level marketing not only for security and independence that I couldn't find in the workplace, but also to be around positive people. Most people involved in multi-level marketing are *very* positive. In fact, I met my wife Becki because of it.

I was working as a computer technician when a cousin introduced me to multi-level marketing. What impressed me was that I could remember when my cousin had been financially broke. When I saw how successful he had become in multi-level marketing, I figured I could do something with it, too. I worked hard, and after four months I was able to go full-time. And I have been happy ever since.

Becki worked with the Social Security Administration for 19 years but makes more money now in MLM than she did working for the government.

One of the greatest things about MLM is that *everyone* has a chance to be successful. Even if they don't feel that they have the qualifications to do well, if they are persistent with their efforts, they *can* achieve their desired success level. Nothing is more rewarding than helping people who are convinced that they cannot be successful to do well!

Here is a simple message that, once again, you will have to reword to fit your product or service:

"You have reached the (your name) hotline number. Through the (your service, product, business, or program), you instantly have over (number) products available to you. I'm talking about quality products you purchase every month at guaranteed lowest prices (savings). In addition to the lowest possible prices, you automatically receive a 100 percent money-back guarantee on all items that you purchase.

"If you're considering the purchase of a (your service or product), let me show you how to purchase it at a substantial saving. And that's just for starters! If you are looking for an unbeatable opportunity to enjoy additional income while being backed by a company with combined assets of over (number) million dollars, at the sound of the tone, leave your name and number and the best time to reach you by phone. I'll get right back with you to answer any additional questions that you might have."

At the end of this message list the names and phone number of two or three associates that your prospects can call if they want more information. Ideally, the associates responding to the message should be in separate downline organizations. This way you build profit in several different lines of sponsorship at the same time.

It is important that there be a set time for the prospects to call for further details. For example, "For further information call Joe Smith, Monday through Thursday evenings between 5 and 7, or call Mary Jones Monday through Friday mornings between 9 and noon."

This is a great way to prospect! If you can't find other associates to work with you on this, promote the program on your own. At the end of the two-minute message, ask prospects to leave their names and phone numbers on your own answering machine.

When you and your associates return calls to the potential customers or prospects, be prepared with a script that fits your business. Include information about your company, the products and/or services offered, and *why* they should buy them from you.

The purpose of this script is not only to briefly inform the person you've called about what you have to offer, but primarily to set an appointment to personally see them and make a sale.

It is *so* important to invest time in this system. It is vital that you work with your associates to help them develop their telephone skills, and that you teach them the most effective ways of setting appointments.

The usual mistake in using a program such as this is to simply hand the scripts to associates in your downline and tell them to "go to it!" It's important to give them the initial support that they need to get them started.

Listen to your associates as they receive phone calls and set appointments. You may only need to do this for an evening or two. This will give you an opportunity to make suggestions and help your associates to simplify their wording and improve their tone of voice and closing phrases. Your helping hand will build their confidence—*and* your business.

You are like a supervisor; double-check to make sure that your business is running smoothly and properly. One of your key objectives is to assist your associates in setting appointments.

Most of the appointments will be set on a one-on-one basis. They may meet the prospects at their home, at the associate's home, or at a neutral location such as a local fast-food restaurant. When a large number of phone calls are being received, it works better to meet with two or three prospects simultaneously. Besides being a great time and energy saver, enthusiasm breeds enthusiasm!

Remind your associates that the purpose in answering the phone calls is not to build interest, but to set an appointment, period!

The purpose of the appointment is not to build interest and/or educate your prospect about your business. The purpose is to make a sale and/or to sponsor your prospect.

Don't misunderstand what is being said here. Yes, it is important to demonstrate your product or how your service works. It is important to discuss the features of your product or service. It is important to give a presentation. But it is *most* important that you lead your prospect toward an involvement with you and your business—by making the sale.

Another idea that has worked extremely well for many associates is to wear a badge or button. This button may be two or three inches in diameter, and have a catchy phrase on it to cause people to ask about your product or service.

Bumper stickers, with your name and phone number printed on them, have also worked well for some networkers.

Realize that all the world is a store of people who are prospects for your product. It doesn't matter how you get the word out about what you are doing, just that you do so.

MLM Success Profile:
The Gary and Faye Burke Story

Prior to getting involved in multi-level marketing, Gary Burke was a coach on the University of North Dakota football staff. His wife, Faye, was in data processing with the control data corporation.

Gary had a strong desire to earn a higher income and was looking for an opportunity, when someone showed him the Shaklee multi-level marketing program. As Gary says, "I saw that, through the magic of duplicating myself in MLM, I could earn an income that would be three to four times my current salary.

"It is interesting that I was attracted to multi-level marketing because of the potential income, but honestly, the pleasure has come from being involved with people. The financial and material rewards have actually become by-products of the process of building our MLM organization. While we immensely enjoy these rewards, they have not been the focus of our efforts.

"Faye and I work out of our home and enjoy managing our time and schedule so that we are able to spend more time with our daughter, Rachel. Also, we take time to play golf on a regular basis.

"We have earned and enjoyed company-paid trips for our entire family to Washington, D.C., San Francisco, London, San Juan, Acapulco, Monte Carlo, Toronto, Montreal, Hawaii, Switzerland, and Germany, as well as to many other beautiful locations." These fabulous trips are rewards for teaching and motivating others to build their business. It is a special thing to be able to have a positive influence on other people's lives.

"As Shaklee Master Coordinators, we have also received free automobiles as incentives, along with an income well in excess of $200,000 per year!"

Gary and Faye's Keys to Success

During our first four months in multi-level marketing with Shaklee, we spent extra time studying our company's products and its opportunity to see how we could do it to our best advantage. Multi-level marketing was new to us, and I knew from my coaching experiences that it was very important to develop a game plan to go along with consistent effort.

We set personal goals and standards that challenged us to not be satisfied with meeting just minimum requirements. We have a very strong belief in the ability of others to duplicate the process.

We have learned that much of our job is to move people from being spectators to participants and finally to their becoming personally involved with the business. This means that it is important to learn to work with the various personalities of people.

It is important to focus on finding solutions instead of dwelling on problems. We have a clear focus on our commitment to our company as well as our own personal business. It is important to stay on track with a quality company and spend your energies looking for new ways to influence people in a positive way.

We cannot stress enough the importance of consistent work efforts.

Chapter

8

FIVE WAYS TO MOTIVATE YOUR DOWNLINE

People who become leaders do so because, at some point in their lives, they decide to. They may have been inspired by some other person, event, or new-found desire, but the bottom line is that they decided to take on a leadership role. In most cases, what it boils down to is that they decided to do something special with their own lives.

You personally may have already made a decision to do something special with your life, but if you haven't, why not do so now? Talking specifically about multi-level marketing, let other people's success inspire you to do better. Take on the attitude that "if they can do it, so can I!" Decide that you also *deserve* to do well with your life.

One of the keys to growing and developing into a better leader is observing others who are doing well in your business. Learn from their mistakes, and, of course, learn from their successes. Ask questions. Write down notes on phrases and techniques that they use to move other people to action.

Be Yourself

For you to become a better leader, be yourself. You do not need to become like some other person whom you perceive to be a leader. There is no question that you could probably improve your ability to motivate others, but don't try to take on another personality.

Let's take a real-life example and show you how two different people with two different personalities can solve the same problem with two different techniques. The situation is that Jane sponsors Bill into an MLM business. Jane has been holding meetings for Bill at his house, and has attempted to get Bill to participate with her in the meetings.

Jane's objective is to help Bill take on more responsibility and thus begin to take over the leadership of his downline organization. The problem is that Bill refuses to do part of the meetings. Jane has observed one of her upline leaders handle a similar situation, which will be explained in Example 1. Jane felt that the technique used in Example 1 could not fit her personality, so she reworked the technique to fit her leadership style, as explained in Example 2. As you read these two examples, the point is that "there is more than one way to skin a cat," and if your desire to do something special with your MLM business is strong enough, you will find a way to overcome your obstacles.

Example 1

Jane observed an upline leader, Charlie, holding meetings for Richard. Charlie, who held several meetings for Richard, had a technique for transferring leadership to downline associates and decided it was time to do likewise with Richard.

What Charlie did was to simply schedule a meeting for Richard at Richard's house, and then Charlie did not show up! He did not call to forewarn Richard, because he figured that Richard would then postpone the meeting until a later date. Charlie knew that with guests in his home, Richard most likely would go ahead with the meeting, thus realizing that he *could* do meetings without Charlie's assistance. He also knew that he ran the risk of offending Richard, and that possibly Richard would even quit the business. Charlie felt that this was a risk he would have to take to see how serious Richard was about the business.

Whether you agree or disagree with Charlie's technique is not the issue. The issue is that Charlie used this technique very effectively many times in transferring leadership to other people. The technique worked for Charlie, but you have to rework it to work for yourself.

Example 2

Like you, Jane realized she needed to transfer leadership to her downline people from time to time. Jane did not feel comfortable with Charlie's techniques, so she accomplished the objective of transferring leadership in a different way.

Jane arranged a meeting for her downline associate, Barbara. The meeting was set for 7:30 p.m. At approximately 7 p.m., Jane called Barbara and told her that a problem developed that would prevent her from attending Barbara's meeting that evening. Before Barbara could say anything, Jane told her that she would do well with the meeting on her own and that she would call her near the end of the meeting, around 8:30 p.m., to answer any questions the guests might have.

There are two things that Jane did here that are significant. One is that she waited until 20 to 30 minutes before the meeting to notify Barbara that she would not be able to attend. The second thing is that she told Barbara that she would make a backup phone call to answer questions. This would help Barbara to realize that she still had support.

In either example, the downline was motivated to take on a leadership role. You will figure out what technique will work best for you, but the important thing is to realize that you can lead and motivate others. You just need to decide that your life is special enough to ask other people to grow in *their* responsibilities just as you are growing in yours.

Five Steps to Becoming a Leader

Step 1: Set Definite Goals

This first step is a most important one; that is, to set a definite goal. What is something that you believe should be done in your and your family's life? If you really believe that this goal is worth the effort, do not let go of it until you achieve it. Try and try again until you accomplish what you are setting out to do.

> *Many are stubborn in pursuit of the path they have chosen, few in pursuit of the goal.*
>
> Friederich Nietzche

You say, "I've heard this before." That's fine, but do you apply what we are talking about here? To build a business you have to have a goal or "reason why" that is strong enough to make you follow through with such enthusiasm and extra effort that you cannot help but grow into a leader.

The point here is that you will have some disappointments from time to time. Most of them will be minor, but occasionally you will have a more significant disappointment.

At moments like this, you hurt. Sometimes you hurt so badly that you feel like quitting your business completely. This is a time to find someone you can talk with in confidence. Someone who will help you sort out your feelings and frustrations.

There is a question you should ask yourself near the end of each week. Where and with whom should you work during the coming week? When you have set a definite goal—one you strongly believe in—the answer will be "where and with whom I can develop the most business." Setting meaningful goals motivates you to work more profitability.

As Dale Carnegie once stated, "Show a man something he wants, and he will move heaven and earth to get it."

There are two main points that are very important here:

1. Setting goals for yourself
2. Helping your downline associates to set their goals

When you are focused on and working toward a definite goal, a higher percentage of your downline organization will be more active in reaching the goals they set.

Most people have a difficult time setting formal goals. With them, you will normally help them most with a "dream session." To help someone dream is to suggest general goals without being specific.

Show travel brochures that include dream vacations. Show brochures featuring new cars, new homes, new boats, jewelry, or clothes. Pass these around for people to look at. Dreaming is very effective, especially when working with a number of associates at the same time. With many people, their goal has grown from just wanting a new object (home, car, or furniture) to wanting a better life style.

In *Think & Grow Rich*, Napolean Hill explains that "definiteness of purpose" is a major fundamental to becoming successful. He also explains that most men do not become successful until after age 50. One reason for this phenomenon is that when you are younger you have plenty of energy to run here, there, and over yonder. As you get older, you have less energy, and nature itself forces you to focus on your goals with a definiteness of purpose greater than when you are younger. If you are younger in age, you just need to realize that it takes more discipline to harness your energy and focus on your goals and objectives.

Why We Joined MLM
Harold and Marcile Hartman, Kansas

I was in row-crop farming for years before going to work as a technician in electronic engineering for an aircraft company in Kansas. I had never been in any type of sales before, but when I discovered multi-level marketing, I liked the idea of setting up other associates and earning money on the wholesale business that developed. I work our MLM business like a major department store, setting up associates instead of stores to distribute our product.

It's important not to listen to the people who say it won't work. Keep talking to the people who are successful and who build you up. My wife, Marcile, is one of those people, and she is 100 percent behind me. After two years with my present MLM company, I have doubled the income that I made at the aircraft company, and therefore have been able to take an early retirement.

Our income comes from associates throughout the United States, Canada, and Puerto Rico. We like being our own boss, and we enjoy the fun of the traveling that we can do because of it.

Step 2: Act Like a Leader

Take charge. Involve others in your project or business. Help those who are willing to help themselves. In other words, stay away from those who are looking for a *handout*, and go with those who will *work out*. Be a leader with the objective of assisting others to become independent. Instead of doing work *for* them, work *with* them to reach their objective.

Most importantly, be yourself. You may be very outgoing, or you might have a more quiet nature. Either way, you must learn to move others emotionally. Let people feel your enthusi-

asm for your business. This enthusiasm can be outwardly exciting, or it may be more quiet. The key here is not which way
you should express your enthusiasm, but that you *do* express it
in your own natural way.

Don't be afraid to step away from the crowd and lead
others. You may do this by just jumping in and taking over a
meeting, for example, or you may start out more gradually. A
simple way to do this is to take on more responsibility in your
business step by step. As you do this, you will become more
and more involved until you reach a point at which it will
become necessary to delegate to others.

As you take on more responsibilities, don't worry about
what others think. No matter how well or poorly you do, some
will think well of you, and others will not. As you make mistakes, learn from them and grow. As others see you learning
from your mistakes, they will grow in their respect for you.
Also, many others will become challenged to grow personally,
as many of them will take on the attitude that, if you can do it,
so can they!

As you read this chapter, you may or may not be able to
visualize yourself leading others. If you do, great! If you don't,
work on it. There are a number of things you can do that will
create an atmosphere that will prompt others to look to you for
leadership.

1. Make copies of testimonial letters, newspaper articles,
   and other materials to hand out to your downline regularly.
2. Call people to let them know about special meetings,
   guest speakers, and anything else that might benefit
   them.
3. Call associates in your downline who are working at
   holding meetings and offer to assist them or to see
   individual prospects with them. You do not have to
   hold the meeting in this case. Just being there, talking
   with prospects, sharing testimonials, and encouraging
   them to get started in your business will be a great help
   to your downline.
4. Introduce yourself to guests at the meetings and say
   good things about their sponsor and upline.

There is a saying that it's the little things that count, and it is just as true in business. You gain the respect of others by respecting them and by providing good service and assistance.

One of the better leaders I ever observed was a gentleman who had an eighth-grade education. This person built a very successful MLM organization by telling others that if *he* could do it, *they* could do it. He told everyone that they could do a better job than he did. He rarely spoke at meetings, but he had one of the most solid and profitable MLM organizations that anyone could wish for. He led others by encouraging them to take on the leadership responsibilities that he felt uncomfortable with.

Step 3: Develop Good Habits

This step requires some common sense, some observation of others, and a little discipline. Each of you has some good habits and some bad habits. Some need to be improved upon, and, of course, some do not. Whatever you feel your weakness is, if you will work on it, it will become one of your strengths. The key is to recognize this weakness and consistently develop it into a good habit.

Let's discuss a few good habits that will benefit you:

1. *Answer questions.* There are several important guidelines here. Once you answer a question, it is best not to become silent; instead, continue talking briefly on another subject that will help keep them thinking about things that are most important to their career. For example, Jane asks you a question about the best time to call prospects during the evening hours. You reply, "Normally, Jane, just after dinner time up to around 10 p.m. By the way, do you know the date of the next rally?

2. *Be personal.* Touch people emotionally. Learn to develop the habit of smiling more often, the importance of making eye contact, and the importance of a firm handshake. These are all basic habits that normally can be improved upon.

3. *Provide a choice of two.* Instead of asking others to do something at a specific time, offer them a choice. By offering them a choice of two times, or two days, or two locations, for example, you will find that a much higher percentage of people will do things you ask them to do.

4. *Live up to your expectations.* A common mistake made in multi-level marketing is to do too much for your downline. It is important to realize that people will tend to live up to the expectations you set for them. Read carefully, as those expectations most often fall into one of two categories. The first category is where the majority of associates you work with do little or nothing. Here are some reasons why:

a. You offer to do meetings for them any time, and attempt to be available at times convenient for them.

b. If they are busy, you ask them to give you their prospect list, and you will call the names on the list for them. You tell them that you will sponsor the prospects for your associates.

c. You tell them to bring a list of names over to your house (or you go to their house), and you will make phone calls to set appointments for them.

d. You tell an associate everything you know about building the business.

e. You tell them to send prospects out to meetings and you will sponsor the prospects in their name.

As you read this category, you probably observe that, by following this train of thought, you will have a large number of people doing little or nothing. Why? Because you did not expect them to do anything. They consequently live up to your expectations. If you are willing to do it all for them, why should they expect to do anything for themselves?

The second category is where a high percentage of associates you work with become very active in the business. Here are some reasons why:

a. You create a sense of urgency in setting up meetings with your associates. You give them a choice of two times. You develop a reason for them to get started immediately.

b. You ask them to make the initial phone calls to their prospects and then you will help them follow up to sponsor them.

c. You tell associates the basics they need to know about building the business. You then tell them that, as you see them doing these things, you will teach them more.

As you read this second category, you hopefully noticed an attitude that required your associates to do something in order to gain assistance from you. The ones that *do* respond will begin to live up to your expectations.

5. *Use language leverage.* This is a very simple concept. You use physical leverage to move heavy objects, why not use language leverage to move people? The choice of two methods we just discussed is a form of language leverage. Use the following phrases to help you move others.

   a. This may not be for you, but it's worth looking at.
   b. Interesting, isn't it?
   c. You like to earn money, don't you?
   d. This is a great value.
   e. Feel–felt–found. When people give you an objective, use the feel–felt–found solution. "Jane, I know how you feel, I felt the same way once in a similar situation, but do you know what I found out?
   f. This makes sense doesn't it? Well, you will find that what you are hearing will make sense to many of your friends also.
   g. On this marketing plan you will remember many of the figures, but not all of them initially. The main thing you should remember is that the more people you involve, the more money you will make.

Why I Joined MLM
Glenda Schneider, California

I am a naturopathic doctor, which involves my doing extensive personal counseling and nutritional work with my patients. My MLM business gives me the latitude to do my counseling and teaching and to do my business on a much larger scale than ever before.

The only financial limits I can see with multi-level marketing are those determined by my own efforts. The fact that other people can add to your income is a great benefit. Putting in extra effort helps you to grow faster. Also, I learned to focus on what my company has to offer. Sometimes people don't realize that they are getting off track with their business in nonproductive ways.

> I have found it very effective to teach people that I'm connected with as much about the product and company as possible. The more understanding and belief they have, the more desire they have to share that knowledge.

As you read these examples, you should be getting the idea. Be observant of others, and you will notice many of their good habits as well as some of their bad ones. Either way, take note, and discipline yourself to add to and improve upon your good habits. Just as you can exercise physically to tone up your muscles, you can exercise mentally and emotionally to tone up your personality and abilities to deal with other people.

Step 4: Grow in Wisdom

It is important to develop the ability to read people and to have a basic understanding of what's going on around you. You will encounter problems, but, by growing in wisdom, you will learn to defuse sticky situations.

One of the better ways to grow in wisdom is to associate with others who are doing well. Attend their meetings. Invite them to lunch. Offer to pick up guest speakers or drop them off when they need transportation. Stay after meetings and talk with them. The point is, you are influenced by your environment, and through associating with other successful people, you will grow in wisdom by observing how they interact with others.

Another great way to grow in wisdom is to read books and magazine articles about other successful men and women in any type of business. If you keep yourself receptive, you can learn from their experiences. Successful people do the things that unsuccessful people fail to do. As you associate more closely with them personally and read about them, you will become more motivated to grow as an individual.

Develop the habit of talking about productive subjects. Remember, people with great attitudes normally talk about ideas; people with average attitudes talk about events; and people with small attitudes talk about other people! Learn to replace the negative words *criticism, condemnation,* and *complaint* with the positive words *conviction, courage,* and *commitment.*

No one is perfect, but it makes good sense to grow in wisdom and mature in your abilities to deal with others. You are not born with wisdom; you acquire it by picking and choosing those people and habits that you wish to emulate.

As we grow in wisdom, we come to the understanding that sometimes we make the mistake of trying to motivate people to be what *we* want them to be, instead of helping them to become what *they* want to be. This point is illustrated in a story about a football coach who had a very successful field-goal kicker on his team. This field-goal kicker was one of the best, as he would consistently kick field goals from the 40-yard line. He *liked* to kick field goals. One day the football coach decided that he would like his star 160-pound field-goal kicker to begin participating in tackling practice with his 260 pound linemen. You can imagine the rest of the story. After a few days of tackling practice, guess who quit the team? The star field-goal kicker!

Find out what a person's interests and talents are, and encourage them to be the best they can be by using whatever talent they possess.

Step 5: Duplicate Yourself in Others

Have you ever seen a turtle sitting on top of a fence post? Probably not, but if you ever do, you will know that it didn't get there by itself. You are more likely going to get to the top by building others up. Take the attitude that you will assist them in building their business, and, in doing so you will build your own.

A big key to building others up is recognizing and complimenting them on their efforts and achievements. People will jump through "hoops of fire" for recognition. With just a little common sense you will realize that it is a good idea for your downline associates to be getting their share of the center stage at meetings. Compliment others to build them up. Good recognition is, in many cases, even more motivating to people than money. Lao-Tzu once said, "Avoid putting yourself before others and you can become a leader among men."

Realize that you cannot *make* anyone successful. You will learn to work with those who will continue to work. This is because you can only help those who have a desire to help themselves. You need only a few people in your downline to follow your example.

How do you pick key people to work with? You don't, they pick themselves. How? By their activity. When you discover people who are trying, regardless of the success they are achieving, it is worth spending some time with them.

Who is a key person? Someone who brings guests with him to a meeting. Look at what people are doing instead of listening to what they are *going* to do. Sometimes, the more people talk, the less they do. This can result in increased frustration for you. Whether they talk a lot or not, look for the activity and results, and then you can decide where to spend your time. "We are so busy getting people in the business that we forget to put the business in the people!" Think about this statement. It makes a lot of sense to help a few people to develop a deep commitment for your business versus a lot of people with just a surface interest.

It is important to realize that you don't build your business on the people you know. Instead, you build *through* the people you know. The reason you sponsor people personally is to reach people they know who will be sponsored downline. The point is, the people *you* know will lead you to people *they* know.

Why We Joined MLM
Tom and Suzanne Atkin, Florida

I got into multi-level marketing shortly after college. During this time I met my wife-to-be, Suzanne, who was also in multi-level marketing. Along the way, I owned two different companies and later worked as a publisher's representative. I have found that some of the greatest sales-attitude training programs are in multi-level marketing.

We believe that it is very important to be persistent in building your business. It is obviously very important to find a good company that has products that give you repeat orders. Developing the ability to recruit others will give you the freedom and independence that you are looking for. Once you get your organization growing, it's a *great* feeling!

You are not in the business to *make* the individual you personally sponsor successful. You are in the business to *assist* him or her to become successful. But, if that person is not responding, then build *through* them with someone downline. You are looking for the person who wants to do well in your business.

The methods you are using to build your business must be duplicable. You, for example, may be able to hold people's attention at any opportunity meeting for two hours, but most of your downline will not be able to. Therefore, discipline yourself to holding opportunity meetings that are 45 minutes to one hour in length. You might say that your meetings are like training birds: if the masses aren't pleased, they will fly away.

If a business-building method is working for you, keep doing it. Another way of saying this is, "If it ain't broke, don't fix it!" The most effective long-term form of management is "leadership by example." It is much better to show them than to tell them.

What you are reading here is that many people are overly concerned about how they can teach others and move others to do the business when they should be more concerned that they themselves are doing the basics. Again, lead by example, and watch for those people who are trying to emulate you. As you find those people who want to learn from you and duplicate what you are doing, work and spend time with them. One of the best forms of exercise you can get is lifting others up! Remember, in multi-level marketing it never fails that, when you help someone else, you will also help yourself.

It is important to realize that there are some basic tasks in the MLM business that you will do better than others. It is just as important to realize that you should not expect to become an expert in all phases of multi-level marketing.

Thomas D. Bailey said, "Conductors of great symphony orchestras do not play every musical instrument; yet through leadership the ultimate production is an expressive and unified combination of tones."

You may not be good at holding opportunity meetings, for example. That's okay. Instead of developing yourself to be great at holding meetings, learn to develop others in your downline to be great at holding meetings. They are the orchestra—you are the conductor.

Some leaders do not like to personally sell products and services. They prefer instead to motivate and train people to build up downline organizations. But many of the leaders have learned the basics of selling so they can lead others into selling the products and services their company has to offer.

MLM Success Profile: The Richard and Andrea Ellis Story

"I wasn't really looking to join anything when I was first introduced to Herbalife by my cousin. I knew nothing about multilevel marketing, and my initial interest was only to try the products. But I had a business of my own that had developed problems beyond my control, and I was talking to an attorney about possible bankruptcy," relates Richard Ellis.

"I used the products, and I began telling people about them and also about the opportunity to earn money. Most of our friends told me they thought I was nuts, but I was determined that nothing would stop me from making a success of my MLM business. No matter what came up, I kept my blinders on and just kept working.

"My company's marketing plan allowed me to start when I was broke and scared. For less than $100 I had an MLM opportunity and could grow as much as I desired. If it had taken a lot of money, a certain background, or experience, I would have been excluded. When I told others about the income opportunity, I did find people who were either willing to trade spare time to earn extra income or willing to work even harder to become wealthy.

"Being new to MLM, my wife Andrea and I were amazed at the incomes we saw being earned by very average people, both full- and part-time. At a point in time we came to understand that it was because their incomes were collective efforts from the organizations of associates they had built. I gained confidence that Andrea and I could also become successful in this business by becoming involved with the support system that my sponsor, other associates, and the corporate home office provided," Richard says.

"Multi-level marketing has been an incredible experience. It has allowed Andrea and I to work hard and earn a very good living, while permitting us to regain both our self-respect and our self-esteem. We ended our first year by earning $75,000, and we've earned close to $1 million during our first five and a half years with our MLM business.

"A really special aspect of the business is the wonderful people we have met and the close friendships that have been formed," Richard continues. "The rewards have been numerous. We have traveled extensively to Australia, Bermuda, Mexico, Canada, the Hawaiian Islands, and all through the United States. To say that this business has been life-changing for me and my family would be an understatement!"

Richard and Andrea's Keys to Success

Multi-level marketing can be a simple business when we apply common sense. I believe that a person must have a personal desire to improve both financially and personally. There needs to be a willingness to work, and the following keys are from a proven plan of action.

1. Do the basics *consistently*. This includes using the products, because this will give you the confidence you need to talk to people about them.
2. You must promote your products and opportunity by talking to a lot of people. Start where you are most comfortable, whether it be with people you already know, or with fliers, ads, or other methods. The key is in the numbers and increased activity.
3. When you are new, make up in numbers what you lack in skills. You will get better with practice.
4. Learn how to teach people how to teach. Lead by example.
5. Set your goals high, but be realistic.
6. Monitor your results, and make adjustments as needed. Results—that's the name of the game!
7. Create a local support system for your organization

and take full advantage of special events, especially those sponsored by your company.

8. Put your best effort into whatever time you have available to build your business. It's not so much the amount of time you have available—it's more what you put into your time that counts.

9. Focus on your strengths and what you *can* do; do not focus on your weaknesses and what you *cannot* do.

10. Do not be distracted from your daily method of operation. Maintain a level of business activity just as you would if you had a boss looking over your shoulder.

11. Maintain the highest values of honesty and integrity.

12. Consistency and persistence are essential for any level of success.

13. Care more about your customer's getting results than about the profit from the sale. Proper follow-up and service will result in a customer base that you can build a solid retail business on. This philosophy is just as true in working with your associates and helping them to become profitable.

14. Patience + patience + patience = endurance.

15. Your attitude is your most important business asset. For example, care about your retail customers. It will determine how you relate to all other aspects of your business.

Chapter 9

HOW TO REVIVE DROPOUTS

Multi-level marketing, just like any other business field, has its heroes. Some of these associates were successful almost from the beginning, and, of course, there are those who struggled before finally reaching financial independence.

Many of the most successful networkers got off to a slow start, but, through persistence and perseverance, eventually did extremely well financially.

Courage and perseverance have a magical quality, before which difficulties disappear and obstacles vanish into air.

John Quincy Adams

In most cases, there was someone upline who took a personal interest in them, answering questions, sharing ideas, and offering encouragement.

It is a good idea for you to find yourself a mentor to study, but it's a better idea to *become* a mentor for others to follow. Most people would like to do well. Show them what to do, be their helping hand, and you can make the difference in their lives.

No matter how great a leader you are or become, you will have associates who become inactive. No matter how wonderful your business opportunity is, some people will become discouraged for one reason or another. This is the nature of the business. Accept this fact, and don't take it personally.

It is normal to feel guilty when some of your associates don't do better than they do. When this happens, double-check to see if improvements could be made in the way you conduct *your* business. If improvements are called for, make them and then continue on, but don't feel guilty.

Remind yourself that no one is perfect. If you are not making mistakes, you are not growing. The important thing is to learn from your mistakes. Look ahead. Focus!

A number of your most successful associates can be developed from inactive people, if you will help them. By staying in contact with inactive associates, when the timing is better for them, they are more likely to become active in your business.

How to Revitalize Inactive Associates

As you continue to sponsor and grow, you should occasionally review your records of associates who are not active. Often the timing will be better for some of them, and they will become more active.

Why is this so? Because in most cases associates become inactive because they are not doing well, not because they lack ability. They may become inactive because of health problems, job changes, lack of maturity, discouragement, negative influences from other people, personal problems beyond their control, financial pressure, divorce, problems with children . . . the list is endless.

Many times the reasons are valid, in others they are simply excuses. For whatever reason, valid or not, the bottom line is that some of your associates will become inactive. Part of your success is determined by how you handle these people.

How to Remove Obstacles that Hold People Back

It is important to understand that all people experiencing discouragement *get* down, but they do not *stay* down. The key is for you to be available when they are ready to begin again. But this takes empathy, and there are some simple keys to be learned here.

One of the most important keys is to not spend a lot of time reviving people. One way to revive others is by staying in communication with dropouts who might later become active. The many different ways to communicate are as endless as your imagination. Rework these ideas to fit both your personality and that of your organization.

Why We Joined MLM
Dominic and Cindy Sitowski, Washington

I was working in life insurance sales, and, because of the large number of people that I would meet, I was approached at least 11 times with an MLM opportunity. Ultimately I decided to join a company under Cindy, who later became my wife.

What I finally saw in multi-level marketing was the ongoing income *plus* the tax advantages. Even though I was making good money in insurance, I eventually realized that I had to start all over each year on a commission income. Multi-level marketing has given us the freedom to dream and then to go out and create the income to make our dreams come true. It also gives us the freedom to be able to take a day off when we want or need to.

It is important to operate your business *as* a business. Look for key people to sponsor. Don't spend too much time with a person who isn't growing. You can have a belief in others, and, to a certain extent, they will live up to that belief. But at some point the people you work with need to make some changes on their own.

Read positive-thinking books and listen to MLM tapes. Doing positive kinds of things will also help you to grow in multi-level marketing.

It is *vital* that you keep a file of your associates, both active and inactive, with their addresses and telephone numbers. I am referring here to your key associates, both personally sponsored and downline.

Approximately two or three times a year, mail something to the person you would like to revive. It could be a copy of your bonus check, a testimonial letter, an announcement that a new product or service is being offered, or perhaps just a short, personal note on a postcard that has nothing to do with business. There are various times of the year that offer natural reasons for you to communicate with your key people, along with key inactive associates.

1. It is a very good idea to do one of these mailings around the last week of December each year. This is the time of

the year when people make New Year's resolutions, try to think of ways to improve their financial situation, and set goals for the coming year. The timing might now be better for them, and possibly they will be open to giving your opportunity another chance. And the opportunity to pay off Christmas bills can be a *great* incentive!

2. The first week of September also seems to be a good time for communicating with inactive associates. Children are back in school, and families are back in a routine. Also, people are beginning to think about ways to increase their income to pay off vacation bills before the holidays.

3. It is human nature to enjoy meeting and listening to celebrities. Every so often you will have a particularly good special guest speaker at a rally. These are events that will motivate and inspire many of your prospects, inactive associates, and active associates to decide to make commitments to get seriously involved by putting forth consistent efforts in building their businesses. Invite your inactive associates to see and personally meet an especially good speaker. They may become inspired again. You never know until you try!

Why We Joined MLM
Phil and Lorraine Poukish, California

I was a retired Air Force lieutenant colonel, and my wife was a registered nurse. It is sometimes difficult for former military people to find good jobs that they like. I had decided that I did not want to get locked into an 8 to 5 routine, and I wanted an opportunity to write my own ticket.

When I first discovered multi-level marketing I saw an opportunity to make big money as well as an opportunity for independence. It has also been exciting making new friends. The quality of people you associate with in multi-level marketing is outstanding.

---

4. Occasionally, you'll receive a new cassette or videotape with an especially inspiring speaker. Lend copies of these tapes not only to your prospects, but to your dropouts as well. Ask

them to listen to the tapes in their car while going to and coming from work.

5. Some people promote a "Fake it till you make it" approach to living. This is where you buy a status-symbol automobile and/or other expensive things hoping that your friends will be impressed by how well your business is doing—whether it actually *is* or not. This is an expensive and unnecessary way to try and build your business, and sooner or later most people will figure out what is really happening.

You will be happier, and ultimately do just as well if not better, with a sincere approach combined with consistent efforts. This approach combined with good service will make you much more relaxed, which will make a definite impression of your friends and prospects.

6. When you are on family vacations, take an afternoon wherever you are to send "what-a-wonderful-place-to-be" postcards to key leaders in your organization, to prospects, and to an inactive associate or two. You will be amazed at how much your postcards will be appreciated and talked about, which helps your business.

You will find that just being yourself is the best approach to working with inactive and active associates. For that matter, you do not need to be hyped up all the time. On the other hand, do not be afraid to let your natural excitement and enthusiasm show. Be yourself!

A critical factor in reviving dropouts is not *their* attitude, but *yours*. If your attitude is one of making a quick buck by sponsoring a few people quickly without providing support, then you will not be around to revive the dropouts. *You* will be the dropout!

Approach your MLM downline associates as business partners. Treat your business with respect, not as a gimmick or a get-rich-quick scheme. This attitude will help you work toward making a good profit now, as well as in the future. Quality attracts quality. With small but consistent efforts over a period of time, you will become like a magnet and attract a higher percentage of inactive associates back into your business than most people.

Stay on Track!

A key here is to realize it is in your best interest for your inactive associates to at least use your products and/or services themselves. Your objective is to be profitable, and, to do so, you will have a mix of business. Some of your downline will be active, some semiactive, and still others will become inactive. The percentage of associates in each category will depend a lot on the stability you personally offer. Other influences include their own personal involvement in rallies and independent seminars.

As in all of life's endeavors, a good example is *always* a good example! But no matter how good an example you set, not everyone is a worker. It is very important to realize that a part of your success is going to be determined by how well you handle those associates who are semiactive.

Treat your semiactive associates with respect. The major difference between them and your active associates is that they have different goals. They may have joined your business only to sell the service or products to make a few extra dollars. Don't sell them short! They *may* get excited later on and really get going.

As you involve yourself with your semiactive associates, it is important for you to keep the "big picture" in mind. Your semiactive associates have a value to you, and the more semiactive associates you have, the more that value is multiplied.

1. Each semiactive associate is a user or potential user of your product and/or service. This business adds up for you, and during many months may be just the extra business volume you need to keep you in the high-bonus level of your marketing plan.

2. Don't judge semiactive associates for just what they themselves might do for your business. Each semiactive associate is a valuable contact who knows dozens of good-quality prospects. Some of these prospects will eventually be sponsored and become good downline workers for you.

Respect them as friends and also for the potential associates they know. Your job is to spend some time with your semiactive associates and help them to sponsor in depth. By working with them, you are more likely—through their contacts—to find at least one person who can become a good worker or leader in each of their downline organizations.

3. Your most profitable MLM leaders readily admit that, in most cases, they did not personally sponsor most of their leaders. Their leaders normally came from the second, third, or even fifth level. Like cream, they rose to the top! Never hesitate to sponsor someone who may become a semiactive associate. After all, he or she may lead you to the person who will become an active associate for you.

4. At some point in time, some of your semiactive associates' personal goals may change, and they could develop into active associates or perhaps even key leaders for you.

Why We Joined MLM
Steven and Beth Trepeck, Florida

I was in merchandising and management with a major furniture retailer, and my wife Beth was a counselor for a health and rehabilitation services agency. After five years on my job, I began to realize that I was very limited as to where I could go to make the type of money that I wanted and yet have the freedom that I desired.

When I first discovered multi-level marketing I was initially looking only to make extra income. Beth and I were pleasantly surprised when we earned more money part-time during our third month in multi-level marketing than she was making in a full year on her job. She was able to leave that job, and later I gained the freedom I was looking for when the income continued to grow and exceed my own annual income from my job.

An important key for us was to keep a positive attitude. Plus we had to be consistent with our efforts, not only when times looked good, but also when they looked bad. Multi-level marketing allows you to live where you want to live. It also allows you to reap the benefits of your own hard work without having the overhead of a normal business.

Whenever we talk to people about our products, we also talk about our opportunity. Almost everyone is interested in making extra income. This has been a real exciting business for us. As people saw us making money, it motivated many of them to join us in the business. You know you have a winner when you can make money, have fun, and help people at the same time.

The Big Payoff

The really big, most profitable associates in multi-level marketing are not people who personally attempted to recruit hundreds of associates. They assisted their personally sponsored associates to recruit hundreds and even thousands of downline associates.

Let's say that you have developed three very active lines of sponsorship, lines A, B, and C. If each line contained two key leaders, three active leaders, and 50 or more semiactive associates, each line of sponsorship would look similar to A's line in the following diagram.

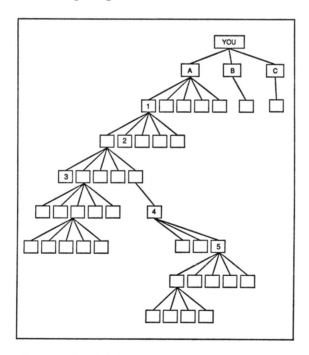

Your desire should be to increase your business. With respect to A's organization, you have a number of options:

1. Work only with A.
2. Assist A in motivating his or her 50 or more downline associates to reach an upper level of the business.
3. Work along with A to assist 1, 2, and 4 to improve their sponsoring activities, the number of opportunity meetings being held, and their business volume.
4. Assist A and 1 to understand the principle of duplication. Based on several factors, including commitment and belief, you should help A to make the decision to work with 3 and/or 5.

Let's say you and A are going to work with 3. This is building a taproot, as described in Chapter 4. You are setting an example for A, 1, and 2 of building depth by working downline from them in one of their lines of sponsorship.

Hopefully 1 will follow the example you set by working downline with 5, thus building a taproot under 4. By working with 3, 1 should be building a taproot under 2.

The point is to focus your efforts with your leaders, but respect the semiactive associates you will be meeting. Respect is having an attitude that does not belittle others or write them off. Instead, if you have respect, you appreciate and accept people as they are.

To tie this example together, you increase your income and downline business through a combination of factors, which includes seeing the "big picture."

1. By respecting your semiactive associates, you stabilize your business with consistent production and usage of your product.
2. By encouraging your key leaders to grow to an upper level of the business, you will dramatically increase your production and profits.
3. By assisting in the development of new key leaders in the downline, you will continue to duplicate yourself over and over. With a good MLM opportunity, when your key people take over the responsibility of leading their downline associates, it means less detail and increased profits for you.

Why I Joined MLM
Joe Boaz, South Carolina

My background previous to multi-level marketing included owning two car-leasing companies. A newspaper ad caught my attention. I went to a meeting out of curiosity, and was introduced to multi-level marketing. Right away I liked the idea that you determine your own success and that the MLM system of duplication can multiply that success.

When you have a genuine first-class product and/or service that fills a need and that almost everyone wants and can afford, then you can be successful! When you help other people, they help you, and, at the same time, everyone can make money. Using people doesn't work. Helping people will get you to the top.

As you accumulate a number of semiactive and inactive associates, you may get the feeling that things aren't going right. When things are not going right, our nature is to not change *people*, but to change the *system*. The larger you grow, the more semiactive and inactive people you will have. The key to holding on to the steady amount of business they do is to continue to develop new leaders to service these people.

When you feel as if you are becoming an inactive associate, talk to yourself as you would a baseball player. All baseball players get into a batting slump occasionally. In this situation, the more inexperienced ballplayers will begin experimenting with new batting stances. It is similar with inexperienced MLM people. When they get into a slump, they may begin searching for that "magic" ingredient.

Experienced baseball players will have batting slumps just as inexperienced players do. The experienced ballplayers, though, know to *return to the basics* instead of searching for some new magic answer. People who grow large in MLM also get into slumps, and like successful ballplayers, they learn to return to the basics of sponsoring, holding meetings consistently, and servicing their customers and associates.

You should be realizing that the semiactive associate that you are reviving may be you. Either way, you will find it most rewarding to lead yourself and your downline back to the basic keys that make MLM work. One of these fundamental keys is to communicate with your existing active and inactive associates, but at the same time, move ahead by sponsoring new associates and help them to develop their downline organizations.

MLM Success Profile:
The John and Sharon Farnsworth Story

John and Sharon Farnsworth have lived in Sandy, Utah for more than 25 years. John and Sharon are a quiet, conservative couple and they are the proud parents of five children. During their years as a family, John has been in business for himself as the owner of an apple orchard on 50 acres of land that surround the Farnsworth home.

The Farnsworths were introduced to multi-level marketing after Sharon became very concerned about her health. A friend of Sharon's introduced her to a company that distributed a line of whole-food herbal formulas.

As Sharon's health began to improve, she discovered that a natural excitement made her want to share her good fortune with others. She discovered that this company had an MLM program. Even though the Farnsworths were new to multi-level marketing, their downline organization steadily grew to more than 12,000 associates!

Sharon says, "In the beginning, we didn't get into this business to make money. Once I began to feel better, I could see how these products could help others. And through sharing with others, we've seen the law of prosperity work in our lives."

As Sharon saw the benefits of multiplying her efforts in multi-level marketing, she set goals for her rapidly expanding group. One of their first goals was to develop an income of over $50,000 per year. They were surprised that in the first year with their company, now renamed Sunrider International, their bonus checks totaled $64,000 for the year. And their annual income has continued to grow.

Year	Total Income
2nd	$104,000
3rd	139,000
4th	250,000
5th	465,000

John and Sharon now have more than 24,000 associates in their downline organization and are executive directors with Sunrider. Besides the high income, the Farnsworths have received four vehicles paid for by the company's incentive program. These vehicles include a Lincoln, a customized Ford van, a Mercedes Benz, and a fully stocked motor home.

"Multi-level marketing through Sunrider has given us the exciting and rewarding opportunity to travel throughout the country, to help others to feel great about themselves, and to enjoy the success and the benefits that come with achieving financial independence," concludes Sharon.

John and Sharon's Keys to Success

We believe that, as you help people get what they want and need in their lives, you receive what you want out of life. The money comes as a natural result of service.

Another key to the Farnsworths' success is talking to people. "When you truly believe in something, you can't keep quiet," says Sharon. "You can't expect people to approach you. Let them know what you have, and then follow through. Keep in touch. Let people know that you really *do* care about them."

Chapter

10

YOUR MLM FUTURE CAN BE FANTASTIC!

Yes, your future can be fantastic in multi-level marketing! It can be a lucrative part-time business or a highly profitable full-time career for each of you who want to be in business for yourself! Consider multi-level marketing as the opportunity to develop a large cash flow with no employees on your payroll. It can be a great way to do business, and a great way to live.

Think of it—you are your own boss. You have no employees to watch over. You have trained and motivated a downline organization that is consistently producing new business and profits for you. You have the freedom to expand your business in a sunny climate during the winter months if you desire. During the summer, you can prospect for new associates and hold meetings in the cool, refreshing mountain areas. You set the location and your schedule. You are now your own boss!

During the holidays, you'll probably be visiting your relatives, right? Why not schedule an extra day or two to plan some meetings to expand your business in the area where you are visiting, and enjoy at least a partial tax write-off? *You* figure it out. Your travel costs are the same whether you hold any meetings or just visit your relatives. The difference is that, if you do some business, you'll have a few extra expenses, but they translate into tax write-offs.

And while you are catching those rays while snoozing on the beach, you are literally "earning money while you sleep," since your associates are continuing to hold meetings that expand not only their businesses and income, but yours as well.

Many people have free time on their hands, but they don't have the income to enjoy this free time. Multi-level marketing can provide that income. Others may have a terrific income, but they don't have the time to enjoy the fruits of their labor. A good, steady income through a solid MLM company will give you additional financial freedom that will help you to eliminate worry and stress.

Many situations occur that will actually work in your favor and help you to prosper in your MLM business.

1. *Recessions and layoffs.* Most people who are out of work are looking for an income. When the economy slows down, MLM activity actually picks up.

2. *Retirement.* Most people who are retiring today need to supplement their retirement income in order to live. Many retirees are more interested in experiencing productive retirement years than in living just a rocking-chair existence.

3. *Job transfers.* Many people today are tired of transferring from city to city. But the major corporations that they work for ask them to make these moves, and, if they want to keep their jobs, they move. A successful MLM business allows you to live where you want to live and how you want to live.

4. *Inflation.* As inflation increases, it obviously costs more money to live. Most people want to either maintain or improve upon their present life style. Multi-level marketing allows you to increase your income whenever *you* choose to.

5. *Taxes.* Many tax advantages result from being in business for yourself and working from your home. CPAs who understand multi-level marketing will tell you that this industry provides some of the best tax write-offs available today.

6. *Working women.* More women are working outside the home today than at any other time in our history. Women who are becoming more interested in marketing are discovering that multi-level marketing is providing them with higher incomes, increased security, and much more personal freedom than if they were working a traditional job.

7. *Busy schedules.* In today's busy society, everyone enjoys personalized service. More and more people are becoming aware of the convenience of the kinds of personalized shopping services that the MLM industry provides.

8. *Now add your own observations.* We all like advantages that work in our favor, don't we? Be observant, and you

will pick up on many new conditions where you live that would make a large number of people more receptive than normal to your opportunity.

Why We Joined MLM
Al and Ora Mae Boardman, Virginia

I was working as a TV service repairman, so we were living on a limited income. I didn't have the capital to invest in a business, but I wanted to increase our earnings.

I saw an opportunity to build a business of my own with multi-level marketing that could give us financial security. We now have a beautiful 4,000 square-foot home with acreage, a really good retirement income, and many friends all over the country. The friendships we have built are like the glue that holds it all together. We enjoy helping others build a second income, and we only work half-days now!

You Do Have a Choice

This is *your* life. You are special! You are not a puppet, although sometimes working a job makes you feel like one. This can be especially true if you have an insensitive boss who is constantly trying to "pull your strings."

If you will but make the choice, you will be quite pleasantly surprised at what special things you can do with your life. Remember, one of the main keys to becoming successful in multi-level marketing is the same as in *any* endeavor—simply start! Just get the ball rolling, and you will rapidly build momentum.

You Never Know Until You Try

You will find direction in your business if you will apply what you have learned in this book. A school teacher once taught me that sustained effort comes from within you. She said that motivation comes "from the inside out," and that it is important to determine to do well. She also taught that the sooner you started a project, the easier it would be to accomplish. In other words, with your MLM business, begin where you are, right now. You don't have to *be* big to *become* big. In multi-level marketing, you become big by building up others.

Encourage yourself to try, or you will never know what you *could* have accomplished. Don't become a person who dies emotionally in their thirties. This type of person usually either just quit trying or lost the hope that something good could happen for them.

> *The wayside of business is full of brilliant men who started out with a spurt, and lacked the stamina to finish. Their places were taken by patient and unshowy plodders who never knew when to quit.*
>
> J. R. Todd

The Boiled Frog Phenomenon

If you put a frog in a pan of cold water and heat the water very gradually, the frog would become accustomed to its surroundings and would just sit there until the water boils. Of course it would die, because it would never become aware of the impending danger.

Now, if you put a frog into a pot of *boiling* water, it would jump out immediately—and survive.

Hang on to your dreams. Don't let your life get into a rut. You've heard what a rut is, haven't you? A rut is a grave with the ends knocked out! Overcome the boiled frog phenomenon!

There are many people who, like that frog, are in such a rut that they won't leave their comfort zone to accept a challenge that would better their lives. They end up missing many of life's great opportunities, including multi-level marketing. Life for them becomes like stale beer, where only every once in a while does a little bubble come to the top and pop. Today, with a good MLM opportunity, your life can be like champagne—and bubble all the time!

Stop and think for a moment. In reality, *you* are the product or service that is to be marketed. You have options and good ideas about how other people can promote services and

products. Why not use some of that same good advice yourself? You encourage others to do things such as complete their
education, change jobs, go out for sports, and reach for the
stars, don't you? Well, why not shake yourself up and follow
through to fulfill your own hopes and dreams?

Being human, you're bound to get discouraged sometimes. But you *can* deal with discouragement. Realize first of all
that you *will* encounter some discouragement in your business,
because discouragement is a natural part of life that is common
to everyone.

So the real question becomes not why do we have to be
discouraged, but how do we deal with it? Learn to let discouragement challenge you, and it will actually help to propel you
forward with your MLM business.

Let's say for example that you have an excellent prospect
for your business. This prospect indicates he will join you in
your opportunity, and this of course excites you. What happens if your top-notch prospect unexpectedly decides *not* to
join you? Of course this can be discouraging, but only if you let
it be. Learn to not let this type of situation become discouraging. Instead, make it a positive situation by asking for referrals.
By doing so, you may end up sponsoring two or three new
associates instead of the one you had originally planned on.
When you ask for referrals, you are more likely to receive them
when you *expect* to receive them.

Some people will try to laugh away your vision. Don't
acknowledge them. Let their ridicule be their own personal
ignorance. If they are not going to pay your bills for you, don't
let them talk you out of a wonderful opportunity that *can* pay
your bills for you. Your true friends will normally be an encouragement to you.

Discouragements will upset you only if you let them!
Choose what you wish to take inside you. Take in what
will inspire you soul to bigger achievements and accom-
plishments, not things that will discourage you. The choice is
yours. You can't sink a ship with all the water in the world unless you let the water get inside the ship, right? Likewise,
no one can sink *you* unless you let the negative feelings get
inside.

Would you let someone come into your living room and dump garbage all over your floor? Of course not! Why then, would you let someone dump garbage in your mind and influence your feelings? People who laugh at you or try to discourage you are in reality only saying "I don't believe that I myself could do this."

Organize a plan of action to help you overcome discouragement and fulfill your dreams. It is natural to feel that some of your dreams are not becoming a reality. In some cases, you planned nothing; therefore, nothing came of your dreams.

Why We Joined MLM
Alan and Barbara Ellis, Indiana

We were introduced to multi-level marketing by my brother-in-law when Alan was selling computer package systems to large corporations in the graphics industry. Alan saw the possibilities in multi-level marketing initially, and I came into the business kicking and screaming! I didn't want to ask my friends for money.

I was in pharmaceutical sales working for large companies, and I had an "image problem" with multi-level marketing.

Alan still enjoys a full-time career in the computer business, but the added security of multi-level marketing takes the pressure off of him when the corporate pressure is on.

And I have the best of both worlds. I like being able to achieve more financial goals with multi-level marketing than were ever before possible. I also like being able to work our MLM business around our two children's schedules. I have better control over my priorities, which are my family, my church, and my business.

We live on a beautiful lake, and I enjoy working out of my home and working together with my husband. With MLM you can set your own pace, work on a part-time basis if you choose, and *still* make better than a full-time income. I feel I'm doing more than just earning a paycheck. Anyone who is serious about working can make money at this business.

Success in multi-level marketing or any opportunity is not necessarily easy, but setting goals together as a family is a good beginning. In some ways, setting goals is similar to taking a vacation. One of the first things you do when you plan a vacation is to decide where you want to go and when. In making these decisions, you are actually setting plans and a date to accomplish a goal.

If you are driving, you will look at a road map to plan the best way to arrive at your destination and will make arrangements for your lodging along the way. This is similar to making a list of names of people to approach about your business and writing down a phone approach for use in calling your prospects.

Examples are used throughout this book to assist you in realizing that success in your MLM business is similar to doing well with other areas of your life. The basic principles are similar.

There is no mystery to building yourself a successful MLM business. There are only basic, fundamental principles that are available to you as well as to anyone who will seek them out. It's up to you whether to remain in your comfort zone, or to move ahead and do something special with your life.

The Eagle and the Oyster Parable

Once there were two eggs discussing what they wanted to be when they hatched. The first egg said, "I want to be an oyster when I hatch. An oyster just lays in the water and never has to make any decisions. The currents of the ocean move it about, so it doesn't have to plan. The ocean water passing by brings its food. Whatever the ocean provides is what the oyster receives, no more, no less."

The first egg continued, "That's the life for me. It may be limited, but there are no decisions and no responsibilities. There's a secure existence controlled only by the ocean."

The second egg said, "That's not the life for me. I wish to be an eagle. An eagle is free to go where it wants and to do as it pleases. Of course it is responsible for hunting its own food and making survival decisions, but it is also free to fly as high as the mountains."

"The eagle," continued the second egg, "is in control, instead of being controlled by others. I want no limits placed on me, nor do I want to be a slave of the ocean. Consequently, I am willing to expend the effort required to live the life of an eagle."

This is a parable with a great point. It is almost always difficult to make your own choices, but what do you want to be? An eagle or an oyster? Do you only want crumbs that others are willing to throw your way, or do you want to create your own destiny?

One of the big attractions to multi-level marketing is that you have the opportunity to "fly with the eagles," but you do not have to burn your bridges behind you to get started.

Remember the "test market" approach (Chapter 3), similar to what McDonald's restaurants and other successful businesses do. When McDonald's restaurants decide to add an item to their menu, they test market it first in a specific area. After the test period, if the new item proves successful and profitable, then they add it to their restaurant chain throughout the country. If the new item does not prove successful, they quietly drop it from the menu in the test market area.

You can take the same businesslike approach to multi-level marketing and give the opportunity a good market test. For once in your life, you can begin to control your thoughts and direct your drive and ambition toward positive achievements.

Sometimes, though, your biggest enemy is yourself. Instead of test marketing a good opportunity that could bring you financial freedom beyond your wildest dreams, you have a tendency to get trapped in your comfort zone in front of your TV set. Sometimes the toughest door to go through is your own. Instead of a door to let you outside, it becomes a barrier that could restrict you to mediocrity.

Break the habit of staying in. Realize that monotony is the "reward" of being too careful or fearful. Challenge yourself to not accept the status quo.

Think about the story of ten soldiers lined up against a brick wall facing a firing squad. The enemy officer in charge offered each of the ten soldiers a choice—face the firing squad and certain death, or walk through a black door in the brick wall. Only one soldier chose to go through the black door!

Why would the other nine choose certain death? Fear! Fear of the unknown that lay beyond that black door.

According to the story as it was told to me, the one soldier who chose the uncertainty of what was beyond the black door received passage back to his army and freedom.

As you read this story, you probably thought that *nothing* could be a worse option than death. You are probably thinking that you would have chosen to go through the black door instead of facing the firing squad. But is that black door much different from your kitchen door? Sometimes you let yourself accept mediocrity in your life instead of pushing through that door to financial freedom.

Pick one solid MLM company and stay with it. There are many people who jump from company to company and opportunity to opportunity. They are on a treadmill going nowhere. They continually gravitate to the newest "ground-floor" idea with a "get-rich-quick" lust. As you read this book, you have seen that MLM can be a great business opportunity, and that there are certain basic business principles that are similar to the MLM industry as to any other business industry. One of these principles is to make a commitment to yourself to find the company that is best suited to you and stick with it. Make time your ally. By sticking with a good company, some of your friends who are watching you grow will join you a year or two later, but not if you are jumping from one company to another.

Just as with any industry there will be fads that come and go. Some of these fads are in training ideas, while others are in marketing plans. Don't be gullible. Stay with the solid leaders of the industry. There have been a number of companies that have paid some famous professional athletes and movie stars an up-front fee to use their name, making it sound as if these famous people are involved with this fabulous new opportunity. This was a gimmick to entice associates to buy some inventory, only to find out a short time later that there was no substance to the excitement.

> ### Why I Joined MLM
> ### Kevin Venner, Texas
>
> As a financial planner, I initially did not realize that I was involved with an MLM company when I purchased a service from a business friend that I later sold to my own clients. After selling 25 memberships, my commission went up. I called my friend and asked him why, and that's when he showed me the MLM opportunity that was available with this particular service. What I saw with MLM was that I could make money by helping other people make money.
>
> When you think about it, a good MLM opportunity makes sense because you can make a profit marketing a company's product, and at the same time remain an independent business consultant.
>
> It is most important to realize that you may not make money quickly in multi-level marketing. Be consistent, especially in the first six months. Overlook the hype as you learn about and develop your business. Don't buy a large inventory of products. Normally you should be able to get started for somewhere between $100 and $500.

Success means something different to each person who seeks it. For some, success is power. For others, it is money in the bank, status symbols, big homes, lavish life styles, or influence. In still other cases, success is peace of mind, living comfortably, security, or any combination of human desires.

Sometimes you will meet wealthy people who are unhappy. Their lives are like a big, beautiful conch shell found at the ocean—beautiful on the outside, but empty on the inside.

And, of course, you will meet many wealthy people who lead very happy and fulfilled lives. Their wealth did not distract from their love for others or their peace of mind. They place a value on their personal lives that wealth adds to instead of distracts from.

Think for a moment about your life and your MLM business in this way. You would like to develop your MLM business so that you can "live beyond the norm," wouldn't you? Most people would consider living beyond the norm, as acquiring a bigger home, a bigger car, and a bigger life style, don't you agree?

Why not consider living beyond the norm in terms of increasing self-control, patience, kindness, gentleness, and peace of mind?

An interesting thought. By becoming more financially independent, you can have more time to spend with your children. You will be able to take them to the park and spend more personal time with them. This will increase the love between you.

More income could also free you from a dead-end job, thus giving you more control over your life. More income could also mean you wouldn't have the pressures of too-much-month left over at the end of your paycheck. This should help you to become a kinder and more patient and kind person.

In essence, when you have your priorities in order, you feel better about yourself. And, when you feel good, normally you are more productive in all areas of your life.

Duplicate yourself. Build others up. The owner of a pro baseball team may pay $100,000 and in many cases much more to their athletes. They look at the fact that, if the athlete performs well, he draws spectators that make the owner a profit on his investment in his players.

The downline organization you develop consists of your players. They make up your professional team. As they perform well, they will make you a profit. Encourage them. Recognize them. Share new ideas, new cassette and videotapes, and books like this one with them. Your objective is to help stimulate them to greater production.

I wish good fortune to each of you. Stay focused on your objectives. Stay committed to the belief that you are special, and that you deserve to live a special life.

There is no question that, in general, people are much happier with a higher income and can handle their problems much better. Also, there is no question that success comes from within you. Success has to do with your own personal self-satisfaction and with how good you feel about yourself, regardless of your material accumulations.

Multi-level marketing can give you the freedom to enjoy your financial success. Start today! Today you can separate yourself from the past or build upon the past. Either way, look ahead. *That's* where you will live your future, and you should desire to live well.

Chapter
11

CHOOSING THE MULTI-LEVEL COMPANY THAT'S RIGHT FOR *YOU*

Some people are very fortunate in that they achieve success with their first multi-level experience.

On the other hand, there are those who do not. Instead, they find the financial freedom and satisfaction they are seeking with the second or third MLM company that they join.

There are also those people who are commonly known in the industry as "MLM junkies." These are the people who join many different MLM companies. In most cases, this type of MLM associate is continually chasing "pie in the sky" instead of making a commitment to work and develop a successful downline business organization with just one company.

The fact that there are numerous multi-level companies to choose from brings up the discussion on how to choose the "right" MLM company. Some people believe that, if you join the right company, then you will automatically make it big financially. This is not a true conception. Companies do not make you successful. Companies offer an opportunity that you can build. You will find that, no matter how fast any company is growing, the people who are moving ahead with that company are doing so due to their personal commitment to extra effort.

So how can you choose a company and know for sure that it is right for you? What are the key factors to look for? How can you even be sure a company will stay in business? Since most of the MLM opportunities *sound* good, how can you make the right decision as to which one to join or stay with?

Although there are no absolute answers to these questions, there are very simple guidelines that you can follow to give you better judgment in your decision-making process.

First of all, if you are happy with your present company, don't become confused when listening to opportunities with other companies, new companies, and/or so called faster-growing companies. Keep the information you receive in perspective. If you've been satisfied with your present company, then strengthen your commitment to that company.

Don't be afraid of missing out on some golden opportunity. Opportunities of one kind or another will always be available. Once again, keep things in perspective. By making a commitment to support your downline organization, the majority of them will make a commitment to you. After a reasonable period of time, if you find that things are just not working out with your present company, then you may feel the need for a move to another MLM opportunity. If you have provided consistent support and leadership to your downline, the majority of your organization will more than likely stay with you.

The point here is that, although it is very important to be connected with a solid company, it is even *more* important that you are providing a solid support system for your downline organization. Don't be too anxious. You will make better decisions by understanding the strengths of your present opportunity rather than joining several new opportunities and looking for a "magic formula."

Why I Joined MLM
Wayne Taylor, North Carolina

Previous to multi-level marketing, I was a Regional Manager with a major company in the health insurance industry. I was also a member of a professional singing group that performed both Gospel and motivational singing.

When I first saw multi-level marketing, I was intrigued with the marketing concept. I saw a great potential for someone who would effectively work at it.

I love the association with people. With a good MLM program and proper training, an average person can build an above-average income.

I don't believe in the rags-to-riches story without work. I do believe that the MLM industry does offer a great opportunity to change for the better the financial lives of people who will apply themselves effectively.

I have been full-time in MLM in one capacity or another for more than six years. Because the MLM industry offers opportunities that are open-ended, anyone can succeed to the level of his or her own energy and creativity.

Let's delve into what you can do to help yourself become more prosperous in your present MLM opportunity.

1. *Friendships.* Build strong friendships, especially with the key leaders in your downline organizations. It's important to have good meetings, good communication, and good support for your people, but sincere friendships are like the cement that holds bricks together.

Stay away from listening to and spreading GOSSIP. Discipline yourself as much as possible to stick with positive and productive conversation. Remember to "put your mind in gear, before you put your mouth in gear."

2. *Support System.* If you are already involved in a good meeting support system, great! If you are not, then look for one or bring others together and develop one.

As you have downline associates sponsored at a distance from you, call your upline leaders or call your company in order to find a good meeting support system for them to join. Your downline associates normally will be more productive when they associate with other motivated people in a good support system. Enthusiasm breeds enthusiasm.

Involving yourself and your associates in a good meeting support system goes along with the leverage principle you will read about in this book. Other people at the meetings will share ideas and information which ultimately assist your associates in building a larger organization. And this will result in increased profits for you. It is important that you look for other committed people to connect with.

3. *Marketing Plan.* Study your company's marketing plan. Understand where the profits come from. It is important to learn how to explain your marketing plan to prospects, but it is just as important to study where you should concentrate your efforts in order to be most profitable.

Typically new associates in MLM have singular vision which consists of sponsoring new people, selling product, and attending meetings. Early in my career, a highly-successful MLM person told me something that really stimulated my thinking process.

He said that he would sit down with a cup of coffee, a piece of paper, and a pencil, and tear his company's marketing plan apart. Then he would study its strengths and weaknesses. He told me that it helped him to see where his time could be spent most profitably.

The point is that sometimes you may feel that you are not earning as much income as you should. Instead of looking at other MLM companies, look at your own first. Find out what you already have. It's probably better than you thought.

4. *Products.* Don't rely solely on a "magic" product. If your company has a number of products and/or services in its line, you will find that, over a period of time, some of them will create more excitement than others. But don't ever forget the basic, solid, repeat items.

If you hear of another MLM company having unusually good success with a particular product and/or service, the odds are that your own company will eventually have a similar product. Ask and find out.

Why We Joined MLM
David and Retta Hall, West Virginia

David works as a supervisor for a major corporation and has always been supportive of my efforts with direct sales. When we saw multi-level marketing, we saw an opportunity to work together.

We saw where we could increase our income through recruiting others instead of just being dependent on what I could personally sell.

We checked into the service that was presented to us to confirm the quality of benefits being offered. We liked the idea of not having products to handle, no paper work to do, and automatic renewals to be paid annually not only on all of our personal sales, but also on sales made in our downline organization.

The key to success in MLM is to help other people. The more you help them, the more they will help you.

---

5. *Company.* It's important to build trust in your company, but don't just build blind allegiance. As you grow with your company, build friendships with key people. This in-

cludes people in the home office as well as with upline leaders who will assist and support your efforts.

Every company will have some problems from time to time. Most of these problems are solveable, and *will* be solved at some point. Unfortunately, some problems will affect you more directly than others. The main thing you need to consider is whether or not your company resolves their problems in a timely and satisfactory fashion.

There are many companies in the MLM industry that are good as well as ethical in their operations. Keep in mind, however, that, as in any other industry, there are those that are not. If you find yourself in a negative situation, cut your losses and move on.

Occasionally you will hear rumors of other MLM companies that are "just like your" company, "better than your" company, or "faster growing than your" company.

So what? It is totally immaterial whether another company is similar to yours. It is also immaterial that someone else considers his company to be better than your company—that's as it should be, after all. And finally, it is totally immaterial how fast any company is growing—even your own!

What is material is that you are *consistently moving forward* with your company. What matters is that *your* own company is providing good support, good products and/or services, and that it has a marketing plan that you find profitable.

At some point it is important to make a commitment. You are more likely to fulfill your dreams with consistent efforts *FOCUSED* in one direction versus scattering yourself in several directions.

For the sake of argument, let's say that you run into the misfortune of being in a negative situation with a company. Are there guidelines that you can follow to help you in choosing a new company? Of course there are!

1. Look for a sponsor you feel you would enjoy working with and who will provide you with a good support system. This doesn't mean that your sponsor needs to be a charismatic meeting holder. It simply means choosing someone that you can count on.

2. When you are looking at a marketing plan, consider the

following:
A. Is the marketing plan simple to understand? Would it be simple to explain to others?
B. Are the qualifications for breakaway levels realistic?
C. Once you develop at least one good downline organization, are the requirements for maintaining a continuing income reasonable?
D. What are the inventory and supply requirements? What paperwork is involved? Who pays bonus checks to the downline organization, you or the company?

Don't be enamored by hyped-up income projections. Look at what is possible with average achievements. If your downline organization cannot achieve fair income levels as they are growing, the hyped-up income will less likely be long term for you anyway.

Why I Joined MLM
Bob Kaiser, Ohio

I have a degree in marketing management and have been involved in retail and wholesale marketing for more than 20 years. For the past six years I have been an independent financial consultant.

My first reaction to multi-level marketing was positive. I liked the principle of duplication. Networking is a much more effective and efficient way of reaching people. Because of the sponsorship aspect of MLM you can see a larger number of people at one time instead of just one person at a time.

There are only so many hours in a day, and this makes it important to be as effective as possible in making your work time quality time. In most conventional opportunities, you present your business program one at a time. Multi-level marketing gives you the opportunity to have your business program presented by literally hundreds of people during the same time period.

I like to sponsor people I enjoy working with. I think it's a compliment to a person that someone would like to go into business with them.

3. Normally, most MLM companies have good products and/or services. Use them yourself before making your final decision to join. Stay away from companies that claim that their products can perform "miracles."

   Check to see what the written buy-back or cancellation policy is. Be very careful about investing in inventory.

4. It is generally rather difficult to evaluate a new company's management and ownership thoroughly. The best way is by not listening to their current projections, but rather by reviewing their past performances.

   Many founders of new MLM companies have a super product or service or idea, but they don't have the experience to handle an MLM organization.

   On the other hand, people who were successful in building up large field organizations are not necessarily qualified to become good administrators or owners of companies.

   And occasionally, there are those founders who do have both the experience *and* the commitment to put a successful business together properly.

   The bottom line is that you don't want to listen to the promises and the hype. A fancy office doesn't guarantee success. You have to observe the overall picture. Do the best you can, and then trust your judgment. Remember, no one has all the answers, not even the owners themselves.

5. The sales aids that will be available to you through a company can be very important to your overall success. For example, if the company does not offer a quality video at a reasonable price, then your sponsoring efforts can be greatly restricted.

   Just because sales aids are available does not mean that you should buy them. But often you need to have more than just a brochure available to you in order to build a successful and profitable business.

6. Timing is important. Is the company growing, stagnating, or declining? Have they added anything that could make an impact for you? If so, how recently?

Are they investing in talented management and new technology in order to stay competitive? Are they committed to quality, service, and good support for you?

Some of the answers you are looking for will not be available right away. It may take months, or maybe several years. In other words, it might take a substantial amount of time for you to see what will really develop.

Consider this. When you think about it, choosing a good MLM company is similar to choosing a career or job with any other kind of company.

If the company is already well-established, you are possibly more assured that they will be in business for years to come. You may have missed the explosive growth time of this company's history, but you can still experience solid growth and financial profits.

If the company is younger, you are more likely to experience rapid growth and advancement, but you must consider the unknown factor of future stability.

Why I Joined MLM
Jack Davidson, Illinois

For 25 years I worked in the marketing industry primarily writing advertising and selling plans for Fortune 500 companies.

After that many years in one industry, my first reaction to multi-level marketing was to avoid it at all costs. I had a bad image of the MLM industry.

My introduction to MLM was as a satisfied retail customer. I was very happy with the products, so I joined the company as an associate in order to purchase my products wholesale. After a while I really looked at the marketing plan and decided to sell the products and sponsor others to pay for what I was using.

Even though I was involved with a good company, I tried a couple other companies at the same time. Unfortunately I wasted a lot of time my first year, because those two companies went bankrupt.

When I decided to concentrate on and commit myself

to my original company, my income began to increase steadily. Now MLM not only provides me with the most satisfactory marketing experience of my life, but also the most rewarding financially.

With MLM I can truly share in a company's profits. And this means much more to me than just collecting a salary. Networking also allows me to build a retirement program along with the true satisfaction of sharing a good product and opportunity with others.

So what can you ultimately do to protect yourself? As you will continually read throughout this book, the major portion of the answer is to treat your MLM career as the business you want and expect it to be. Follow the business attitude of commiting yourself to building a long-term future with your present opportunity, but spend your money carefully and wisely, as expecting it not to last.

For example:

1. Keep your expenses in line. That way, if the company you are currently with develops insurmountable problems, you are not held back with a lot past debt if you find it necessary to begin with another opportunity.
2. Don't spend all of your income on depreciating purchases. Invest a portion of your profits wisely so that you ultimately have something to show for your efforts.

Think about and refer to this chapter as you make decisions concerning your multi-level career. Be flexible as you develop that delicate balance between your business life and personal life. If both are satisfactory to you, then you are more likely to enjoy your MLM career and become successful. Apply common sense to your goals and objectives.

Here are a few suggestions to help you from getting that "burned out" feeling.

1. As you hold meetings in other states and areas, allow time for sightseeing. As the saying goes, "take time to smell the roses."
2. It would be nice to earn over $100,000 per year, and

many people in multi-level marketing do. But keep things in perspective. Your personal financial goals may be more modest. And if they are, that's just fine.

Success isn't totally tied to the amount of money you earn. Everyone needn't be in the top ten to be happy. Financial freedom for yourself is not the same as it is for someone else. What I'm saying is, don't be frustrated if your income goals are not as high as someone elses. Be proud of your own personal achievements.

3. There are highly-successful MLM achievers who still go bowling, vacation regularly, attend church, see movies, go to sporting events, and watch TV. You are less likely to become burned out by maintaining at least some of your recreational activities. It's just as important to work to budget your time as it is to budget your money.

    Don't be afraid to dream, but don't let other people's dreams become your own. Don't be pressured into doing things that are not in your and your family's best interests.

    You will find far less pressure in choosing a multi-level company if you will protect both your money and your time investments.

The Chuck and Charlotte Shelton Story

Before I got into multi-level marketing I sold dental equipment which ultimately evolved into my building my own dental equipment leasing company. Charlotte worked in the bonds division of a bank, and she later became an assistant trader in securities.

When it was first presented to us, Charlotte saw multi-level marketing as a great opportunity, but at first she wasn't interested in talking with our friends about it. But as she saw the value of the products, she became eager to share their benefits with our friends. My initial reaction was that it could give us the opportunity to change our financial life. In the leasing business, we just didn't have the freedom and lifestyle we desired.

For years we had talked about getting out of the city and living on a ranch. Within two years Charlotte and I went from being deeply in debt to buying a 100-acre ranch. Because of the Neo-Life multi-level opportunity, we now own the ranch debt-free and have the freedom to enjoy the forests, creeks, and pasture land along with our Texas longhorns, peacocks, swans, and Canadian geese.

It hasn't all been easy, as we've had challenges to overcome. Some people are skeptical of MLM and of their ability to do it. What I see in multi-level is that one doesn't have to be a superstar in order to do well. Charlotte and I support our downline organizations. We've spent extra time with people when it wasn't profitable, because we knew that once their confidence grew they would develop consistent production and profits for them and us.

We have earned and enjoyed six all-expense paid trips to Hawaii, two to Mexico, trips to Korea, Taiwan, Hong Kong, and beautiful resorts throughout the U.S., as well as a Caribbean cruise. Our favorite trip of all was to Tahiti and Bora Bora.

I was honored to be asked to be the founding President of Neo-Life of Japan spending 1½ years opening that country for our company, and we also have some business in Australia.

We have found that people who fail normally do not have a cause. To earn more money is just not enough of a reason for many people to make a commitment. People are more likely to succeed when they have or develop a purpose, reason, or dream.

Many people in our downline have reached income levels of $3,000, $5,000, $10,000, and even $15,000 per month. We're proud to have so many distributors in our downline organization growing to reach their dreams.

Chuck and Charlotte's Keys to Success

Among the many keys to success, we feel the following six are the most important:

1. For long-term success, a person has to have a quality product or service.

2. It is important that the company and/or company personnel have a proven business track record and proven management experience.
3. A person should be with a company that maintains a highly-respectable reputation in the industry.
4. One should go with a company that is a specialist in the industry, not with somebody who tries to be everything to everybody.
5. It is important to be with a company that does honest research, has its own professional research personnel, and maintains quality control in manufacturing.
6. The company itself as well as its personnel must have marketing integrity and honesty.

We personally believe in the product concept that generates repeat business. Charlotte and I have satisfied customers who have been with us for more than thirteen years.

Caring about distributors, whether they are small or large, helps to maintain consistent business production. It is important to *help* others, not to overload them with products.

Do the little things. These require extra time, but it's time well spent because they will produce extra results.

1. Write personal notes and include them with the bonus checks.
2. Send notes of appreciation to retail customers as well as downline distributors. Include *something*—literature, samples, or whatever—in every order that you ship out.
3. Produce informative newsletters on a regular basis.
4. Hold regular meetings. Even when we are out of town, we arrange for someone else to conduct our local meetings.
5. Put yourself in other people's shoes.

There are many other little things that you will learn to do that make a difference, but what it all boils down to is helping others!

Glossary

ASSOCIATES — People who market the product. Also referred to as distributors, representatives, consultants, and dealers.

BREAKAWAY LEVEL — A level of achievement whereby an associate creates an amount of business volume that qualifies him or her to receive the top bonus in a marketing plan.

CROSSLINE — Associates who are sponsored by your upline business associates, not including your own business structure.

DOWNLINE — Associates below you in the business structure, even though they may earn a higher income than you do.

GROUP VOLUME — An associate's personal volume and the personal volume of all downline associates up to a breakaway level.

IN DEPTH — Working in depth means working downline.

MEETING — A group of people getting together to listen to your business opportunity. Also called a seminar, get-together, or function.

MLM — Multi-level marketing.

NETWORKING — Another term for multi-level marketing.

ONE-ON-ONE — Showing your marketing plan to someone on an individual basis.

RALLY — A function normally considered to be motivational. Usually held on Satur-

	days. A rally usually includes a guest speaker, recognition, awards, motivation, and training.
RETAIL PROFIT	The price the associate charges a retail customer for a product less the wholesale price paid to the company or upline sponsor.
SPONSORING	Recruiting new associates into your business.
TAPROOT	A system where you work with and hold meetings for associates who are downline from you, perhaps six or more levels removed.
UPLINE	Associates above you in your business structure.

One More Thing . . .

The MLM industry includes many creative people at all levels of the business. Most of you have an idea, a phrase, a story, a sales technique, or a sponsoring technique that works for you. And if it works for you, it can work for someone else.

There will probably be a follow-up book to *How to Make Big Money in Multi-Level Marketing*. If you would like to share your ideas with me, they may possibly be included in my next book. Of course, you will get the recognition you deserve. Ideas from *all levels* of the business and from *all countries* are welcome.

Please mail to:
Dave Roller
P.O. Box 920688
Norcross, Georgia 30092

When you mail your suggestion, please include your address and phone number so that, if I use your idea, I can contact you personally to verify your suggestions and obtain a release. Each of you deserves recognition for what you do regardless of the size of business you have in the MLM industry.

Index

NOTES

NOTES